"This book should awaken us from our ¡
sacramental, and pentecostal streams
things, but we should not think of the
peting alternatives. Rather, each of these traditions highlights something
essential to full-orbed and flourishing Christian experience. We can no
longer afford to pick one favorite while neglecting what the others have
to offer. This is a provocative call for a fresh ecumenical synergy—for
weaving all these elements together into something stronger and better than
the older, isolating silos were able by themselves to deliver. Ever the pastor-
theologian, Smith concludes with some practical proposals for moving us
in this right direction."

Glen G. Scorgie, professor of theology and ethics, Bethel Seminary San Diego

"In *Evangelical, Sacramental, and Pentecostal*, Gordon Smith is a constructive
provocateur. The word *and* in the title of the book is far from a mere gram-
matical connector. 'And' is indicative of Smith's call to Christians, including
evangelical Christians, to embrace together realities which too often are
considered incompatible with each other, if not denied altogether. Furthermore, this call is not a call primarily to individual Christians or to some
form of private piety. It is a call to churches—a call to churches to be the
church. At the same time, this book is not primarily a critique but an
invitation—an invitation to enter into and celebrate, in Smith's words,
'an ecology of grace.' *Evangelical, Sacramental, and Pentecostal* is a wise and
thoughtful invitation, accompanied by concrete suggestions, for churches
to enter more fully into the grace that is found in union with Christ."

W. David Buschart, professor of theology and historical studies, Denver Seminary

"Christians often live in a state of spiritual malnourishment, choosing exclu-
sively between the Word, sacraments, or renewal by the Spirit. In this timely
pastoral appeal to overcome historical and theological divisions, Gordon
T. Smith invites believers to be drawn into the fullness of life—fellowship
with the living God—by embracing the divinely appointed means of grace."

Jeffrey W. Barbeau, professor of theology, Wheaton College

"This is a timely and significant book because it captures the emerging ecumenical, experiential spirit of our times. Smith's book offers a brilliant and practical vision for how the contours of an evangelical, sacramental, and pentecostal spirituality can be integrated into a full-orbed Christian spirituality and ecclesiology. This kind of perspective is absolutely in tune with what the church in post-Christendom needs in these days when we are redefining our identity as God's people and need resources to help guide us in that important work."

Lee Beach, associate professor of Christian ministry, McMaster Divinity College, author of *The Church in Exile*

"This book is a wonderful corrective to the tendency to be locked into our own theological tradition and be critical of other perspectives. Our Christian communities would be more vibrant and attractive to the unbelieving world if we intentionally incorporated the best in all traditions. Dr. Smith's book demonstrates how this can be done with integrity."

Glen Shellrude, professor of New Testament, Alliance Theological Seminary

EVANGELICAL, SACRAMENTAL & PENTECOSTAL

WHY THE CHURCH SHOULD BE ALL THREE

Gordon T. Smith

IVP Academic

An imprint of InterVarsity Press
Downers Grove, Illinois

InterVarsity Press
P.O. Box 1400, Downers Grove, IL 60515-1426
ivpress.com
email@ivpress.com

InterVarsity Press® is the book-publishing division of InterVarsity Christian Fellowship/USA®, a movement of students and faculty active on campus at hundreds of universities, colleges, and schools of nursing in the United States of America, and a member movement of the International Fellowship of Evangelical Students. For information about local and regional activities, visit intervarsity.org.

Scripture quotations, unless otherwise noted, are from the New Revised Standard Version of the Bible, copyright 1989 by the Division of Christian Education of the National Council of the Churches of Christ in the USA. Used by permission. All rights reserved.

While any stories in this book are true, some names and identifying information may have been changed to protect the privacy of individuals.

Cover design: Cindy Kiple
Interior design: Daniel van Loon
Images: dry brush watercolor: © Liliia Rudchenko/iStockphoto
*   light gray background: © in-future/iStockphoto*

ISBN 978-0-8308-5160-7 (print)
ISBN 978-0-8308-9162-7 (digital)

Printed in the United States of America ♾

Library of Congress Cataloging-in-Publication Data
Names: Smith, Gordon T., 1953- author.
Title: Evangelical, sacramental, and Pentecostal : why the church should be all three / Gordon T. Smith.
Description: Downers Grove : InterVarsity Press, 2017. | Includes bibliographical references and index.
Identifiers: LCCN 2016046949 (print) | LCCN 2016056721 (ebook) | ISBN 9780830851607 (pbk. : alk. paper) | ISBN 9780830891627 (eBook)
Subjects: LCSH: Church.
Classification: LCC BV600.3 .S644 2017 (print) | LCC BV600.3 (ebook) | DDC 262--dc23
LC record available at https://lccn.loc.gov/2016046949

P	22	21	20	19	18	17	16	15	14	13	12	11	10	9	8	7	6	5	4	3	2
Y	34	33	32	31	30	29	28	27	26	25	24	23	22	21	20	19	18	17			

for joella

CONTENTS

INTRODUCTION

I CAN REMEMBER SITTING ON a bus in Lima, Peru, along with others who were attending a conference where I was speaking to a group of theological educators from around Latin America. After we boarded and as we headed to the conference venue, I began chatting with those seated across the aisle from me and learned that they were from an Anglican theological college in Chile. We conversed a little more, and then I asked, "So what is distinctive about the Anglican Church in Chile?" The reply quickly offered was, "The Anglican church in Chile is evangelical, not sacramental." *Interesting reply*, I thought, and while I did not ask it out loud, my immediate thought was, *but do we have to choose?* Why the immediate need to insist it is one and not the other and, in effect, to pit them against each other?

Then later that same year I was in Romania, visiting with the faculty of a Baptist theological college in Bucharest. From there I was scheduled to head across town to pay a visit to the pentecostal theological college. I let my hosts at the Baptist school know where I was headed and asked about the differences between the two schools and their ecclesial families. My host at the Baptist school made it very clear that these were two very different worlds: we are evangelical, they are pentecostal. And in moving between these two "worlds" in Romania, I was reminded of similar contrasts around the world—between Presbyterian and pentecostal in Brazil, or Baptist and pentecostal in the Ukraine, or Methodist and charismatic in Cuba—and how one could easily get the impression that these are two different religious traditions.

I grew up in Latin America, in Ecuador. For my teen years, I worshiped with my family at the Templo Evangelico Alianza, on the corner of Quito Street and Avenida Primera de Mayo in Guayaquil. The church was founded in 1915 and reflects a century of evangelical missionary presence in Ecuador. The pastor who baptized me in that church was the Rev. Miguel Lecaro Tobar. The church was very definitely located, theologically and spiritually, as not sacramental; my baptism, however meaningful, was as much about what it did not mean rather than what it might mean. Pastor Lecaro insisted that this was *not* a sacrament, not a means of grace in itself. And the church was also very clear that we were not pentecostal or charismatic. This was an *evangelical* church, meaning that the heart and soul of worship was the Word preached, and Pastor Lecaro was quintessentially a preacher.

My evangelical heritage typically assumed that one had to choose: *evangelical* meant that you rejected the sacramentalism of not only the Catholic Church but any Protestant church that even seemed to hint at the possibility that the sacramental rites were a means of grace. Further, *evangelical* meant "not pentecostal" in the sense that we were very much a people of the Scriptures—read, preached, studied—and that as such we were suspicious of any kind of experience of a spirit or the Spirit that was not directly mediated through the Scriptures. Tension between Evangelicals and Pentecostals actually came to a head during the second Lausanne Congress on World Evangelism in Manila in 1989, with many pentecostal

Christians actually threatening to leave the conference. With gratitude we need to recognize the huge role that Professor James Packer played in that congress, assuring those present that we are all called, to quote the Pauline line that Packer uses for a book title, to "keep in step with the Spirit."

But do we need to choose? Or can we be pentecostal, evangelical, and sacramental? Indeed, I wonder if we *need* to be, if in fact we want to appropriate as fully as possible the grace of the ascended Christ.

In 1953 Lesslie Newbigin published one of the most important books on ecclesiology written in the twentieth century, *The Household of God*. Ordained with the Church of Scotland, he was writing from Madurai, India, where he served as bishop of the Church of South India. And as many have noted, his unique vantage point from both East and West enhanced his already astute theological insight into the nature of the church, or what it means to be the people of God. In this publication he speaks of the church, in distinct chapters, as Protestant, Catholic, and pentecostal. By Protestant, he meant the Lutheran and evangelical tradition of stressing the importance of faith in response to the Word preached. By Catholic, he meant the perspective that grants the sacraments pride of place in religious life. And by pentecostal, he meant that perspective that stressed, in his words, "experienced effects."

Or, put differently (still Newbigin), in the first, the church is the gathering of those who hear and believe the gospel; in the second, the church is found in sacramental participation in the community that is in historical continuity with the apostles; and in the third, the church is the fellowship of those who receive and abide in the Spirit.

While I am going to use different language in the chapters that follow, I am indebted to Newbigin for the fundamental insight that there are three distinct angles by which we might consider and live in the grace of the ascended Christ. We do not need to choose one of them. Indeed, perhaps it is imperative that we *not* choose but actually embrace and engage each as the necessary counterpart of the other. In other words, not only is it not necessary to choose, it is crucial that we learn how each is an essential means in dynamic interplay with the other, by which we appropriate the grace of God.

This consideration of these three angles or perspectives suggests that there is an ecology of grace—a dynamic, a kind of eco-system, with distinctive contours that brings us to an appreciation of the very way that grace functions, with a generative counterpoint between Word, sacrament, and the immediate presence of the Spirit, with each known and experienced in the fullness of grace precisely because this is how grace works.

Recognizing this requires that we begin where we must begin, with the crucified, risen, and ascended Christ Jesus. The Christian faith is Trinitarian. And yet it is also Christocentric; there is to Christian identity, practice, and experience what Michael Welker aptly calls a "Christological concentration." The goal and dynamic of the Christian life is to be "in Christ." Or, as Paul puts it so eloquently in Colossians 1:27-28, this is the mystery of the gospel, "Christ in you, the hope of Glory." And thus Paul therefore concludes, "It is [Christ] whom we proclaim, warning everyone and teaching everyone in all wisdom, so that we may present everyone mature in Christ." Paul stresses this precisely and intentionally after the hymn of praise to Christ Jesus, whom he describes as the image of the invisible God, the one in whom the fullness of God dwells, and in and through whom God is reconciling all things in heaven and on earth to himself (Col 1:15-20).

Thus the goal of the church, its reason for being, is to live in dynamic communion with its Living Head: growing up into Christ, maturing in Christ, living in real time, organically, in the grace of Christ Jesus.

Paul presumes through all of this something that believers must keep in mind as they consider the grace of God and its place in the life of the church and the world, that everything, literally everything, pivots upon and is drawn up into the wonder of a living, ascended Christ. We begin here; we end here. Christ ascended. In chapters one and two I will be providing a more comprehensive consideration of the ecology of grace in the Gospel of John and the Luke–Acts narrative. And I will be stressing that both the Gospel of John and then the Luke–Acts narrative assume the ascension. Both only make sense in light of the ascension.

And yet the most extended and focused attention to the ascension is found in the book of Hebrews. Indeed, global theologians often comment that the lack of a dynamic theology of the ascension in the life of the Western evangelical church is in part due to a neglect of the book of Hebrews in her preaching and teaching.

In the book of Hebrews, the work of Christ is portrayed as a duality: cross and ascension. Thus Hebrews opens with the ode to Christ that includes the line, "When he had made purification for sins, he sat down at the right hand of the Majesty on high" (Heb 1:3). The same dynamic of cross and ascension emerges again toward the end of the book of Hebrews. "Looking to Jesus the pioneer and perfecter of our faith, who for the sake of the joy that was set before him endured the cross, disregarding its shame, and has taken his seat at the right hand of the throne of God" (Heb 12:2).

Jesus, to whom we look, is the pioneer and perfecter of faith. He is a pioneer in that he goes before us, leading the way, establishing the path and the example. We *follow* Jesus. But he is also perfecter in that through his work, he makes possible our following.

Thus the Christ Jesus who is profiled in the book of Hebrews is the *ascended* Christ. And more, what defines the Christian life is our participation in the life of the ascended Christ. The ascension becomes the dynamic focal point for the Christian life and experience, as the book of Hebrews make clear early on in those tremendously comforting words:

> Since, then, we have a great high priest who has passed through the heavens, Jesus, the Son of God, let us hold fast to our confession. For we do not have a high priest who is unable to sympathize with our weaknesses, but we have one who in every respect has been tested as we are, yet without sin. Let us therefore approach the throne of grace with boldness, so that we may receive mercy and find grace to help in time of need. (Heb 4:14-16)

Jesus is spoken of as the great high priest who has passed through the heavens (Heb 4:14). This is the identity of Christ—crucified, yes, but crucified and now ascended. It is this dynamic between cross and ascension that, in effect, defines the Christology of this book in the New Testament.

In other words, in the book of Hebrews, the salvation of God is not defined solely and narrowly as something that is transacted for us, external to us and then applied or imputed to us.

Yes, there is an external action; yes, and, of course, this external action—the cross of Christ—defines all of history and defines our lives. Everything depends on this: Christ, in the language of the book of Hebrews, "endured the cross." And yet it is a truncated gospel, a partial and incomplete gospel, if our understanding of the cross is not anchored in both the incarnation that set it up and the ascension that gave it ultimate meaning.

And the emphasis on the ascension reflects a particular vision of the Christian life. Fullness in Christ, maturity in Christ—the goal or telos of the Christian life—is to be drawn into the very life of God.

We are taken up in Christ, found in him, participating with him and thus able to enter—in him and with him—into the holy place. We become partakers of Christ (Heb 3:14 KJV).

The question this book considers is precisely this: *How* do we become partakers, entering into the grace of the risen and ascended Christ? How and by what means are heaven and earth transcended and the grace of the crucified and ascended Christ made available and appropriated by the church and by the individual Christian?

By "the grace of God," we mean the liberating assurance of forgiveness. We mean the capacity to live in peace, love, and joy—the huge longing of the human soul. We mean actual divine strength that infuses our human frames and makes us capable of living the Christian life. Most of all, by "the grace of God," we mean the capacity and experience of life in Christ—for the individual Christian and for the church. And this assumes, of course, that the Christian life is not self-constructed, but lived in response to the grace of God and in dependence on the grace of God. The church is not self-constructed. It is quintessentially the fruit of divine initiative and grace.

In what follows, I will begin with the Gospel of John and ask, with particular reference to the intriguing line in John 15:4, not only what it means to "abide in Christ as Christ abides in [us]" but specifically how this grace, the grace of being "in Christ," is even possible and how it is to be sustained. Then I will do the same for the Luke–Acts narrative to demonstrate along similar lines how the church is to remain in dynamic communion with the risen and ascended Christ. As I trust will be patently evident, both the Gospel of John and the Luke–Acts narrative signal or indicate that our union with Christ can be understood as evangelical, sacramental, or pentecostal, or, more properly speaking, that both New Testament texts assume it is all three.

In chapter three, I will bring the three together and do two things: profile how the significant voices of John Calvin and John Wesley might speak to these questions and also show how the three might be considered together and why they each matter, together. From there, I will proceed to a full chapter on each, where I will consider this question: So then, at root, what does it mean to speak of the church as evangelical . . . as sacramental . . . as pentecostal?

THE EXTRAORDINARY
INVITATION OF JOHN 15:4

JOHN 14–16 ARE TYPICALLY SPOKEN OF as the "upper room discourse," and aptly so. At the conclusion of his earthly ministry, immediately prior to the cross, Jesus is in an intentional teaching mode with his disciples. Readers sometimes miss, though, that the teaching of Jesus in these chapters sets up what is to follow: Christ Jesus will be ascended; following the death and resurrection, Jesus will be returning to the Father; and the disciples need to be ready for this new reality.

The character and manner of their relationship with Christ will be altered. Big changes are coming. They will no longer see Jesus, hear him, or touch him. Well, they *will* hear and see and touch, but the terms of their relationship will change and change significantly.

The high point in these comments—everything prior to John 14 and 15 leads up to this declaration, and everything that follows, in the rest of John 15 and into John 16, fleshes it out further—is the extraordinary invitation of John 15:4, when Jesus says to his disciples with intimacy, power, and purpose: "Abide in me as I abide in you."

This remarkably simple invitation captures the heart of the matter. It was to this end that Christ came as the incarnate one; it was to this end that Christ is moving to the cross. The intent is not merely that they would be saved from their sins. In one sense, of course, that was the agenda. But to what end? This salvation means that Jesus' disciples would find in Christ their true home even as they learn to be the one in whom Christ dwells. And Christ dwells individually—personally, as the dynamic of their faith and experience—and collectively, for the church finds its true identity as the community that abides in Christ as Christ abides in the church.

Admittedly, it might be a challenge for many if not most of us to get our minds around this. What does it mean to abide in Christ as Christ abides in us? What does Jesus envision when he says this to his disciples?

Our answer comes by two things that Jesus offers the original disciples. The most obvious is that Jesus gives the disciples an image, a picture by which they and we can get a sense of what Jesus means. He speaks of the vine and the vine-grower and of being grafted into the vine. It is a compelling image that is familiar to most if not all readers of the New Testament. Jesus speaks of God the Father as the gardener in this extended metaphor. Jesus himself is the Vine. This is so very significant; the original disciples would have assumed Israel was the vine. Now Jesus declares to them that he is the vine. And that is a clear reminder to the contemporary Christian that in the end, the church, however vital to the purposes of God and essential to what it means to live in the vine, is not to be confused with the vine. Jesus is the vine. And then—the point of the metaphor—life is found and fruit is borne as the disciples are "grafted" into the vine, that is, into Christ Jesus himself.

We would ideally feel the full force of this: our lives are so interconnected with the life of Jesus that we cannot be explained; we do not live, except by dynamic and essential communion with Christ. We quite literally draw our life from him; we live not merely by virtue of what he has done for us in the past but further that now, by virtue of the cross, we are being drawn up into the life of Christ and the life we live we live "in Christ."

And then, second, Jesus offers something that may be even more powerful and compelling, though less obvious perhaps on first read. We see that the vision of the Christian life to which we are called in this text is dynamically portrayed to us—subtly, but powerfully—through the lens of the life of the triune God. What Jesus does here is simply breathtaking. And it must not be missed, else we do not feel the force of what Jesus calls us to in John 15:4.

John 14 is, in the estimation of many, the great Trinitarian chapter of Holy Scripture. Jesus makes it as clear as possible that he and the Father are one yet distinct and that his life, as the Son of God, is intimately one with that of the Father—as Jesus abides in the love of the Father and does the will of the Father. Indeed, he even says something that clearly anticipates John 15:4, when he observes that "I am in the Father and the Father is in me" and then he speaks of "the Father who dwells in me" (Jn 14:10-11).

But then, just as the reader is beginning to make some sense of that, we have the stunning revelation that there are not two but three: Jesus will not leave his disciples orphaned, but promises instead to send the Holy Spirit, a theme that is then picked up again in John 16.

Furthermore, Jesus speaks to the unique fellowship, or communion, that exists within the Holy Trinity, a communion where to know the one is to the know the other two. What demarcates this extraordinary relationship, Father-Son-Spirit, is love. The whole description of the dynamic of the Trinity in John 14 ends with the words that Jesus has said and done all that he has so that the world would know that he, Jesus, loves the Father (Jn 14:31).

The ancient church had a particular word, *perichōrēsis*, to describe this union of love, this giving and receiving of the triune God. It is a word that is unique to the fellowship of the Trinity, and it has been sustained in our theological lexicon through the Eastern Orthodox tradition. It speaks of the wonder of the most beautiful thing of all, the glory and wonder of the triune God, Father-Son-Spirit, living in dynamic and life-giving community, sustained by the love they have for the other.

Then we come to John 15 and the call of John 15:4: "Abide in me as I abide in you." And what captures our imagination is that Jesus portrays the dynamic of this call, its essential elements or features, through the same phrases that Jesus has just been using to describe his relationship with the Father within the Holy Trinity. As Jesus abides in the love of the Father, we are to abide in the love of Jesus. As Jesus lived by the word and will of the Father, so we are called to allow his word to abide in us and to live as those who do his will.

In other words, in some mysterious way, the phenomenal intercommunion of Father, Son, and Spirit sets the stage for the fellowship that *we* have with Christ. And our appreciation or understanding of the Trinity is the lens through which we are to consider our relationship with Christ. We enter into fellowship with Christ—abiding in him—and we are drawn into the life of the triune God, individually and corporately, as the church.

Both of these images call us to a realization that the Christian life is defined first and foremost by *union with Christ*.

Thus three things call for special emphasis. First, the animating dynamic of the Christian life is not a Christological principle or a doctrine about Christ, however important it is for us to have an understanding of Christ Jesus that is faithful to the Scriptures and to the Christian tradition. Rather, what defines us, animates us, not merely informs but transforms us, is Christ himself who in real time dwells in our midst and in our lives.

Second, it is therefore very important to stress that the heart and soul of the Christian existence is not ultimately about being Christlike, however much that might be a good thing. It is rather that we would be united with Christ. So much contemporary reflection on the Christian life speaks of discipleship as becoming more and more like Jesus. There are two potential problems with viewing this Christlikeness as the Christian ideal and the goal of the church. On the one hand, this is problematic because Christlikeness is derivative of something else, namely, union with Christ. And to pursue it on its own actually distracts us from the true goal of the Christian life.

And then also, when Christlikeness is the goal, we get caught up in debates about what Christlikeness looks like and so easily the church descends to a less than subtle form of legalism as we impose on the church a vision of what it means to be "like Christ."

And then third, so much piety, especially in evangelical circles, presents what might be called a transactional understanding of Christian spirituality—that Christ has "transacted" something on our behalf. While Christ has definitely acted on our behalf, it was to an end; his actions, notably his death, were not an end in themselves. The purpose of the cross was not merely about a transaction, effected for us and for our salvation. The cross had a purpose, an intended outcome: namely, union with Christ.

So we have the call "abide in me as I abide in you" (Jn 15:4). We have the image of the vine and the powerful references to the intimacy and fellowship within the Trinity. But we still have the question. How is this even possible? Christ is the ascended Lord at the right hand of the Father. And we are invited—called—into this union with Christ, a union anticipated in the amazing encounter Jacob had with heaven—the ladder, between heaven and earth, between God and humanity, between Christ Jesus and ourselves.

How can heaven and earth be transcended? How can we, mere mortals, be in dynamic fellowship and union with Christ, Lord of heaven and earth, one with the Father and the Spirit?

In the history of the church there have been three defining and paradigmatic answers—three answers that have in their own right each had a profound influence on the church and what it means to be the church. Three answers: the evangelical, the sacramental, and the pentecostal. And for each, the case can be made from the Gospel of John that this is indeed the answer to the question of how we can speak of mutual abiding in Christ.

All three answers or responses presume the cross. They each assume the passion of Christ (Jn 19). Each only makes sense in light of the work of Christ as the crucified one. But then we are asking this: Given the cross, how is the grace—gained, one might say, on and in the cross—effected in our lives? How are the saving benefits of the cross made available to the church and to the world? How is this grace available and actually effected in the life of the individual Christian believer?

THE EVANGELICAL ANSWER

How can Christ abide in us even as we abide in him? How can we speak of this mutual co-habitation, so dynamic that it can be thought of as comparable in kind to the mutual love and fellowship that is found within the Trinity? The evangelical response is simple: Christ abides in us through the Word of God, most notably through the Scriptures read, studied, preached, and meditated upon. It is the Word that transcends heaven and earth; it is by the Word that we are drawn into fellowship with Christ and thus with the triune God.

Evangelical tradition sees John 15:4 through the following series of considerations. First, an evangelical would note that the call and invitation, "abide in me as I abide in you" is quickly followed, just a few verses later, with the words, "if . . . my words abide in you" (Jn 15:7), which seem to echo the language of mutual abiding.

For some, that settles it; the Word is the means by which the church abides in Christ. But the theme of the Word and words, the words of Jesus, run like a river through the whole of the Gospel of John. The Gospel opens with a magisterial declaration of the centrality, priority, and glory of the Word. The second person of the Trinity is the very Word of God, the one through whom all things were created, echoing the stunning language of Genesis 1: God spoke and all things came into being. So now in John 1, the Creative Word comes to us as the Redemptive Word.

Then also, this Word, the Logos of God who was with God and then who we read is very God of very God, comes to us as Jesus, a Rabbi and our teacher. Indeed, Jesus self-identifies in John 13:13 as Teacher and Lord. This is not unique to John's Gospel, of course; all four Gospels reveal Jesus as a teacher. Jesus is one whose ministry is the ministry of the Word, stressing in Mark 1 that his vocation, his calling, is to teach.

What must be stressed, however, especially from a reading of the Gospel of John, is that the word spoken by Jesus is a redemptive word: it is nourishment for the soul; it is the very means by which the salvation of God, the grace of God, is known. The disciples of Jesus, he says, are those who "continue in my word" (Jn 8:31). They know the truth and the truth makes them free (Jn 8:32).

A disciple of Jesus is one who hears the teaching of Jesus, leans into and believes this teaching, and then obeys and lives the teaching. A disciple is drawn into the very life of Jesus by this intimate living of Jesus' teaching. And this continues with the ascension; Jesus urges his apostles to continue his ministry with the call of John 21 to Peter in particular to "feed my sheep" (Jn 21:15-17). This is clearly in explicit continuity with Jesus, who in the prayer of John 17 speaks of those who will believe in him through the word of the apostles. It anticipates what is evident throughout the New Testament: the church is a teaching-learning community. This teaching is in continuity with the ministry of Jesus as a teacher and indeed the teaching ministry of the church is the ministry of taking the words of Jesus and making them present in preaching and teaching to the church of each generation. The church is fed—sustained—by the Word of God read, taught, preached, heard, and lived. All of this is the context and background for appreciating the words of John 15:7, "if . . . my words abide in you."

Thus we come back to John 15:4, "abide in me as I abide in you." How is this even possible? How can we envision this and then move into and live in this dynamic relationship of union with Christ, the ascended Lord? The evangelical answer is, through the Word. The Christian is one who feeds upon the Word, the Scriptures, and the church lives by the preaching of the Word. The faith of the church is sustained and strengthened by the Word.

THE SACRAMENTAL ANSWER

How do we abide in Christ as Christ abides in us? The sacramental response sees a different thread—well, not a thread but a river—that runs through the Gospel of John.

The sacramental Christian is equally taken with the grand opening of the Gospel of John: in the beginning was the Word, and the Word was with God and the Word was God (Jn 1:1). But from a sacramental perspective the great and climactic moment comes later in the first chapter of John with the stunning declaration of John 1:14 that speaks to the moment when everything changed radically, thoroughly, and permanently: "And the Word became flesh and lived among us . . ."

The entire course of human history was radically altered. When we ask how we can be in dynamic communion with the Lord of glory, abiding in Christ as Christ abides in us, the sacramental Christian sees a one-to-one link between John 1:14 and John 15:4. It is by and through and in the incarnation of the Word that heaven and earth are linked, dynamically and thoroughly; this is the means by which the grace of God responds to the crisis and fragmentation of the created order.

God in Christ assumes, that is, takes on, materiality. Our physicality becomes his home, his tabernacle. He took on our flesh so that, as Paul puts it, we might become children of God (Gal 4:4-5). God became one with us so that we might become one with him. The genius of this event is that the stuff of creation—the physical, the tangible—becomes the very means by which God unites us with himself in Christ.

For the sacramental Christian, then, physical and tangible things can be and indeed are a means by which we are drawn into the life of God. This is possible only with the incarnation, of course. And that is precisely the sacramental point: with the incarnation, the very matter that God created is a means of grace by which creation is healed.

Thus the sacramental perspective comes to John 3 and reads that we are born anew, born from above, "of water and Spirit" (Jn 3:5). And for this perspective, Jesus' words are clearly and obviously a reference to water baptism. Water, the very stuff of creation, becomes a means by which we are drawn into the life of God and rebirthed. The water itself has power, or, more properly speaking, the water has power as linked with the ministry of the Spirit. As the words of the Gospel of John make clear, it is water *and* Spirit. For the sacramental Christian, while fully affirming the vital role and place of the Spirit and how the water is a means of grace with the Spirit, water is yet very much a means of God's grace.

Then also, the sacramental perspective comes to the phenomenal words of Jesus in John 6—troubling words to the original disciples and perplexing for many on first reading, when Jesus uses rather graphic language to speak of what it means to live as his disciples. He stresses, starkly and without compromise, that a disciple is one who eats the flesh of Jesus and drinks the blood of Jesus. "I am the bread of life" Jesus insists; the bread that he gives, for the life of the world, is, as he puts it, "my flesh" (Jn 6:48, 51). And then in words that for the sacramental perspective clearly anticipate John 15:4, we read, "Those who eat my flesh and drink my blood abide in me, and I in them" (Jn 6:56).

In response, many if not most evangelical Christians have insisted that this is all metaphorical speech and that is speaks only of an interior "spiritual" eating. But the sacramental Christian responds with perplexity and not a little consternation, insisting that to the contrary, the language of John 3 is clearly the language of water baptism, and the language of John 6 clearly speaks of the Lord's Supper, the Eucharist.

For the evangelical, the church is a teaching-learning community that lives by the Word preached. For the sacramental Christian, the church is a sacramental community, the gathering of the baptized, who live—are sustained, and abide in Christ as Christ abides in them—by the bread and cup of the Holy Meal. Furthermore, they are organically linked to one another as a community by the apostles. In other words, our sacramental connection is not only to bread and cup but in the shared communion at the Table, there is a fellowship with the rest of the Christian community, the church, and with the apostles who founded the church.

Thus the incarnation becomes the means by which we live the words of John 15:4, and this finds continued expression in the church through baptism and the Lord's Supper.

THE PENTECOSTAL ANSWER

How can we abide in Christ as Christ abides in us? Those of a more pentecostal or charismatic perspective observe the following: the great means of connection—between heaven and earth, between God and humanity—is the gift that Christ gave the church and each Christian, the gift spoken of in both John 14 and 16, the gift of the Spirit. The gift of the Spirit, they note, bookends the call of John 15:4. It is the Spirit who will lead the disciples into understanding and truth (Jn 15:26; 16:12-13); it is the Spirit who will glorify Christ in the life of the disciples (Jn 16:14).

This emphasis on the Spirit is also a thread that runs right through the book of John, beginning with the opening chapter. The sacramental Christian looks to John 1:14 for the great turning point of John 1: the Word became flesh. For those of the pentecostal persuasion, the pivotal moment of John 1 comes later in the stunning words of John the Baptist when he declares, "I saw the Spirit descending from heaven like a dove, and it remained on him. I myself did not know him, but the one who sent me to baptize with water said to me, 'He on whom you see the Spirit descend and remain is the one who baptizes with the Holy Spirit'" (Jn 1:32-34). In the parallel passage to this, Luke 3:16, John the Baptist speaks of how he baptizes with water but that there is one among them who will baptize with Spirit and fire.

For the pentecostal, the whole point of the coming of the Messiah is Pentecost, the outpouring of the Spirit upon one and all. But more, the Spirit is then the very means by which believers know the grace of God.

In John 3, the salvation of God is known when one is born from above, born of the Spirit—which for the Gospel of John is one and the same. The intervention and gracious power of the Spirit makes God's salvation known.

So then it follows, at the grand conclusion of this Gospel, that we come to the stunning moment when Jesus commissions his disciples with the call: "Peace be with you. As the Father has sent me, so I send you," and he empowers them to fulfill this very call with his own breath. He breathed on them, we read, and then declared, "Receive the Holy Spirit" (Jn 20:21-22).

Thus for the pentecostal, if we ask the question, how do we abide in Christ as Christ abides in us? the answer is simple: by receiving the Spirit, being born from above by the Spirit, and being led into truth by the Spirit, Christ abides in us.

WHICH IS IT?

So, how do the church and the individual Christian dwell in Christ? How does this dwelling, both call and invitation, actually happen?

Is it through the Word—the ancient text, made present and effective through teaching and preaching?

Is it through the sacramental actions of baptism and the Lord's Supper, as it would seem to be the case from a reading of John 3 and John 6?

Or is it through the immediate presence of the Spirit in the life of the church and filling—breathed upon—the individual Christians?

The response of course is that it is not either/or but all of the above. And the three ways are not all of one kind.

But it remains to demonstrate further that all three in tandem are the divinely appointed means by which God's people live in union with Christ.

All three, taken together, are the means by which the benefits of the cross are known and experienced. The three—Spirit, along with Word and sacrament—are then the means by which the intent of the cross is fulfilled in the life of the church, the means by which we abide in Christ as Christ abides in us.

Jesus makes the specific point that his disciples will only bear fruit, fruit that would last, insofar as they are grafted into the vine. Thus it only makes sense that we would embrace every possible and God-given means by which we could be living in the vine and bearing the fruit to which we have been called—individually and in the life and witness of the church.

Each is essential if we are to embrace the words of Christ: in and through him our joy is made complete (Jn 15:11).

TWO

LUKE–ACTS: THE SPIRIT AND THE LIFE OF THE CHURCH

THE CHURCH LONGS FOR the grace of God to be present—a transforming presence—in the life of the church. We long for the church to be a community of the "graced ones"—graced by God who has acted for the world and for the church in Christ Jesus.

In this exploration of how the grace of the risen and ascended Christ Jesus is made present and effective in the life of the Christian community and thereby through and in the world, this chapter asks, what, according to Luke–Acts, does it mean for the church to be a graced community?

Three observations stand out for further investigation. First, the grace of God in Christ is clearly in and through the Holy Spirit. We note this powerfully not only in the life of Jesus himself, in the Gospel of Luke, but then post-Pentecost in the life of the church and thus all Christians. And this is why, no doubt, those within the mystical, charismatic, and pentecostal church traditions have always relied heavily on and appreciated this portion of Holy Scripture.

Second, the ministry of the Holy Spirit must be understood in light of the pivot on which all history rests and turns: the ascension of the incarnate, crucified, and risen Christ.

And third, our understanding of the ministry of the Spirit needs to be located within the life and ministry of the church. The Spirit's ministry is very ecclesial; it is churchly. Ecclesiology and pneumatology are intimately linked. The Day of Pentecost is the day of the church; the work of the Spirit is the fruit of and evident in very specific church practices.

Thus, exploring these first two observations will speak of the Christological character of the ministry of the Spirit; exploring the third will profile the ecclesial character of this ministry.

JESUS AND THE SPIRIT

First, consider the relationship of the Holy Spirit to Jesus—coming to this connection from the vantage point of the question, how is the church a graced community? The book of Acts clearly testifies that the church was a graced community. But doubtless the Gospel writer Luke intended the book of Acts a volume two of a longer narrative: that is, the book of Acts must be read in light of the Gospel of Luke. The experience of the Spirit in the life of the early church is an echo, a counterpart, to the experience of the Spirit of Jesus that is described for us in the Gospel of Luke.

In the Gospel, the Spirit plays an intimate, dynamic, and powerful role in the life of Jesus. Indeed, from the conception of Jesus to the promise of the Holy Spirit at the end of Luke, there are eighteen specific references to the Spirit.

At the conception, we read that the Spirit comes upon Mary at the conception of Jesus and then also upon Elizabeth, Mary's cousin. "The Holy Spirit will come upon you . . . the child to be born will be . . . [the] Son of God" (Lk 1:35). And it is Elizabeth, who, in the fullness of the Spirit according to the text, declares of Mary, "Blessed are you among women, and blessed is the fruit of your womb" (Lk 1:42). And exquisitely, a man named Simeon, described as one on whom the Spirit rested, was led into the temple to meet the newly born Christ-child.

When we consider the life and ministry of Jesus in the Gospel of Luke, we see that Jesus' ministry is very much "in the Spirit." The sequence begins with the reference to the descent of the dove in Luke 3:22; the Spirit leads him into the desert—Jesus, "full of the Holy Spirit," "was led by the Spirit in the wilderness" (Lk 4:1). Then we read that Jesus, "filled with the power of the Spirit," returns to Galilee and commences his teaching ministry (Lk 4:14). And when he comes to the synagogue, he confesses that the "Spirit of the Lord is upon [him]" (Lk 4:18). From there on, throughout the Gospel of Luke, we see numerous additional references the Spirit, including the intriguing reference of Luke 10:21 which describes Jesus rejoicing "in the Holy Spirit."

All these references point to an immediacy of the Spirit in the life of Jesus. Luke is stressing this—highlighting it, speaking of Jesus filled with the Spirit, empowered by, guided by, and rejoicing in the Spirit.

But it does not end there. From the life and ministry of Jesus we begin to look to the disciples. Luke stresses that this same Spirit is granted to Jesus' followers. Early in the Gospel we have John's (the Baptist) remarkable words that the one who is coming—the Messiah— will baptize with the Holy Spirit and fire (Lk 3:16). Then also there is the intriguing, almost passing, comment of Jesus that the Father will "give the Holy Spirit to those who ask him" (Lk 11:13). And then we have, of course, the grand conclusion of the Gospel of Luke that includes the promise of the Holy Spirit in Luke 24:49: Jesus will send upon his disciples the promise of the Father; they will be clothed with power—a power that is from God.

ASCENSION-PENTECOST:
THE COUNTERPOINT OF THE COSMOS

When we make the transition from Jesus to the church, from the Spirit in the life and ministry of Jesus to the Spirit in the life and ministry of his disciples, there is a pivot on which this transition rests and turns: the ascension.

The ascension is vital to Luke's theology of the Spirit and his understanding of the life of the church. The Gospel of Luke concludes with a reference to the ascension: Luke 24:50-51—Jesus blessed his disciples, lifted his hands and, we read, was carried up into heaven. Then, the book of Acts opens with the ascension. Indeed, there are three references to the ascension in Acts 1 and 2. What is apparent to us is that if we take Luke–Acts as one narrative—in two parts, certainly, but still a single narrative—it rests, or pivots, on the ascension.

This suggests that the ministry of Christ will find expression through the ministry of the Spirit. And more, the Spirit's ministry in the life of the church must be viewed through the lens of the ascension. The two events—ascension and Pentecost—are distinct but inseparable.

The ascension is the triumph of God—Jesus is made Lord and Christ as he returns to the right hand of the Father. But it is not the culmination. Pentecost follows, and it must follow for the purposes of the ascension to be fulfilled.

We read in John 14 that the disciples were confused when Jesus told them that he would be returning to the Father. But now after Pentecost, the twenty-first century reader should get it; there is no reason for the church to be confused. We see the powerful link with Pentecost and the outpouring of the gift of the Spirit.

It is noteworthy that following the ascension, Christ is still fully present to his disciples. Matthew's Gospel ends with the assurance: "I am with you always, to the end of the age" (Mt 28:20). Paul—most notably in Ephesians 4—speaks of the church as living in dynamic fellowship with Christ, the ascended Christ, who is the head of the body. And the church is growing up into him who is the head (Eph 4:15-16).

And yet in Luke–Acts it is not merely the ascension that is in view but also Pentecost. What we see and come to appreciate is that the intent and purpose of the ascension is fulfilled in the sending of the Spirit. The grace of God for the church through the ascended Christ is effected in the life of the Christian and in the life of the church through the Holy Spirit. It is the Spirit who equips and empowers the church to live in fellowship with the ascended Christ, and it is by the Spirit that the mission of Christ is fulfilled in the world.

This interplay between the ascended Christ and the Holy Spirit is a very complex one, of course. But at the very least we can affirm the following.

First, our Christology, our theology of the person of Christ, must be thoroughly pneumatological. In other words, we do not have a theology of Christ without a theology of the Spirit. Or, putting it even more bluntly in terms of our experience: we do not have Christ until and unless we have the Spirit. It is by the Spirit that the ascended Christ is present to each Christian and to the church as the community of Christ-followers. There is no experience of the grace of God in Christ except that which is effected in the life of the church through and by the Spirit.

Second and just as crucial, our pneumatology, our theology of the Holy Spirit, must be thoroughly Christological. In other words, the Holy Spirit glorifies Christ in us and in the church. If we have an experience of "spirit" that does not lead us to Christ and dynamic union and fellowship with Christ, then we must ask, what "spirit" is this?

The primary work of the Spirit is to draw us into the fellowship of the Holy Trinity. Through Christ and in glory to Christ, we are brought into fellowship with the Father—Abba Father. And the primary evidence of the Spirit in the life of the church is that Christ is lifted up, to the glory of God the father.

Thus true Christian worship is Christ-centered, not pneuma-centered. The meaning of worship is that the ascended Christ is adored, preached, and encountered in the Holy Meal. In worship we meet Jesus. In worship we have an encounter with Jesus in the power of the Spirit and to the glory of the Father. But the dynamic center and focus is the second person of the Trinity. Our pneumatology is Christological. Thus the ascension and Pentecost are twinned. Each gives meaning and expression to the other. With the ascension, Christ promises his disciples the gift of the Spirit. And very specifically they are urged to wait—or, in the exquisite words of the King James Version of the New Testament, they were to *tarry*. The ascension does not stand alone; it is twinned with the gift of Pentecost and the outpouring of the Spirit on the church. The ascension without Pentecost would make no sense, and in like manner, Pentecost only makes sense in light of the ascension.

So, how is the grace of the ascended Christ made present to the church? How can the individual Christian live in fullness of life under the reign of the ascended Lord? Through the grace of the Spirit—receiving and living in the gift of the Spirit. Ascension and Pentecost are distinct but inseparable.

THE IMMEDIACY OF THE SPIRIT
IN THE BOOK OF ACTS

This emphasis on the connection between the ascension and Pentecost, this insistence that the ministry of the Spirit can only be appreciated in light of Christ and the work of Christ, does nothing, absolutely nothing, to limit the immediacy, presence, and power of the Spirit in the life of the church or the individual Christian.

To the contrary, any reading of the book of Acts leaves the reader with a keen awareness of how the early church was attentive to and responsive to the ministry of the Spirit. And, I would add, to a *sensible* awareness of the Spirit in the life and witness of the church. Note three expressions of this evident presence of the Spirit in the life of the early Christian community: the conscious reception of the gift of the Spirit at Christian initiation, the discernment of the Spirit in the work of the church, and the intentional dependence on the Spirit as the power of God animating the church.

Regarding Christian initiation. Those initiated into Christian faith were expected to receive the gift of the Spirit as, one might say, their birthright. One has a clear sense that the very purpose of the incarnation, life, death, and resurrection of Jesus was that the ascended one could ask the Father to baptize his people with the Spirit. It was to this end that Jesus came. Pentecost was the natural, obvious, and essential outcome of the work of Christ. Thus Paul asked the Ephesian believers if they had received the Spirit in their coming to faith (Acts 19). Receiving the Spirit was taken to be part of what it meant to come to Christ. And when it was evident that they did not receive the Spirit, they went back to the basics of initiation: water baptism and the laying on of hands that they would receive the Spirit.

We read that Peter and John went to Samaria to those who had accepted the Word of God precisely and specifically to lay hands on them so that they would receive the Holy Spirit (Acts 8:17). This expectation also comes through clearly in Paul's experience of coming to faith in Christ. As Luke describes the encounter with Ananias, we read that Ananias actually says the words: he had come so that Paul's sight would return and, most crucially, that Paul might "be filled with the Holy Spirit" (Acts 9:17).

Consider also the experience of Peter with Cornelius. What eventually settled the matter for Peter, what made it evident that Cornelius was with Peter a follower of Christ, was that Cornelius had also received the gift of the Spirit. Peter testified to this when he came before the elders and apostles, noting that God had given to them, the Gentiles, the Spirit, "just as he did to us" (Acts 15:8).

Regarding discernment and the guidance of the Spirit. Clearly the early church responded intentionally to the Spirit. They *attended* to the Spirit: they lived by an awareness of the Spirit in the midst of their circumstances. The Spirit guided them—literally and immediately.

By the Spirit, Philip headed out to meet with the Ethiopian and by the Spirit, Peter and Cornelius came to meet each other. Through the immediate witness of the Spirit, the church in Antioch discerned that they were to set aside Paul and Barnabas to mission work in Asia minor. They were, as the text says so clearly, sent on their way "by the Holy Spirit" (Acts 13:4).

We also see this attentiveness to the Spirit in the deliberative process described in Acts 15, in what is typically called the Council of Jerusalem. The debate and discussion over whether Gentiles need to become Jewish before becoming Christians concludes with this remarkable declaration by James, who was presiding over the conversation: "It has seemed good to the Holy Spirit and to us" that there would not be a Jewish imposition upon Gentile converts (Acts 15:28). In other words, the deliberative process—both in Acts 13:1-3 and then in Acts 15—was one of attentiveness to and responsiveness to the real-time presence and witness of the Spirit among them.

Regarding empowerment. The book of Acts describes an early Christian community that lived by a dynamic that can only be explained by virtue of the immediate presence of God in their midst. Whether it was the "wonders and signs" (see Acts 2:43), or the gracious harmony of mutual love and community, Luke's intent is clear:

the Christian communities described in the book of Acts experienced the transforming grace of God. They experienced something that could not be attributed to anything other than the Spirit at work in their midst.

The genius of the presence of the Spirit in the life of the Christian and the life of the church means that the life of the Christian and the life of the church cannot be explained apart from what is clearly a grace-filled empowerment from God—perhaps even a sensible, or perceptible, empowerment, a deep awareness and heartfelt consciousness that the Spirit is making the Christian a Christian and making the church the church.

The ascended Christ was present with purpose and power in the life of the early church through the ministry of the Holy Spirit.

TWO FUNDAMENTAL ECCLESIAL PRACTICES

And yet that is not the full story, however phenomenal that may seem on first blush. There is another current—or two—running through the Luke–Acts narrative that needs to be recognized and affirmed as we respond to the question, how does the church live in the grace of the risen and ascended Christ?

Toward the conclusion of the book of Luke, the author narrates an encounter that has fascinated the church of every generation and culture. The risen Christ meets two disciples, not of the twelve, on the road to Emmaus (Lk 24:13-35). This is a liminal time, a time of significant transition. Christ has been with his disciples in person, in the flesh. But things are changing. Following his death and resurrection he now meets them in different guise, in anticipation of the ascension. And we can ask, how is Christ present to these two Emmaus road disciples and how might this give us insight into how Christ is present to them and to the church following his ascension? How do they experience the grace of the risen Christ? Could it be that this chapter is very intentionally a transition chapter—a kind of segue between Christ present to his disciples where they could see him and touch him and hear him with their five senses to a new dispensation and a new arrangement wherein Christ is still present, but not in precisely the same way?

We read that the two disciples were disheartened following the crucifixion as they headed home to Emmaus. A stranger comes upon them and they express their disappointment: they had hoped, they tell this person whom they do not yet recognize, that "he [Jesus] was the one to redeem Israel" (Lk 24:21). They had heard rumors of a resurrection but seemed to have dismissed them because those indicating as much were women. (Luke must have had fun with that one!) And in response, we read, Jesus was present to them in two ways, through two distinctive acts.

First, we read that on the road, as they continued on to Emmaus, Jesus began with Moses and then continued through to the prophets, opening up the Scriptures for them to see the revelation of the Christ and the meaning of Christ's sufferings.

Later they would speak of this experience with these remarkable words: "Were not our hearts burning within us . . . while he was opening the scriptures to us?" (Lk 24:32). Jesus had been present to them through the exposition of the Scriptures.

And then, second, we read that they came to their home in Emmaus and they invited Jesus to come in as their guest. But the guest in no time becomes the host and at the table. "He took bread, blessed and broke it, and gave it to them" (Lk 24:30). And later the two who were with Jesus would say to the other disciples that Christ had been made known to them—they recognized him—in the breaking of the bread (Lk 24:31, 35).

We might not make too much of all of this except for what follows when we turn the page and consider the commitments of the early church. Acts 2 is a foundational chapter in Holy Scripture, with Peter's Pentecost day sermon after the outpouring of the Spirit and the outline of the basics of Christian initiation in Acts 2:38 and following. The chapter includes the intriguing reference in Acts 2:42 that those who responded to the preached Word that day committed themselves to fundamental practices: "They devoted themselves to the apostles teaching and the fellowship, to the breaking of bread and the prayers."

I remember as a young pastor enjoying this verse as I preached a four-point sermon on the four practices of the early church, with the observation that the church committed themselves to teaching, fellowship, the Lord's Table, and prayer. It took many years—and I confess it should definitely have not taken so many years—before I saw it: in fact, the text speaks of two, not four, defining practices.

They devoted themselves to the apostles teaching and the fellowship. They were a community of the Word, a preaching, teaching, and learning community; they were the fellowship of the Word. The apostles' teaching was located within the fellowship.

And then, second, they committed themselves to the Lord's Table within and as part of their common prayers. The language of "prayers" likely speaks to their shared worship, very possibly, as some have contended, worship expressed through the Psalms.

They devoted themselves, in essence, to two practices, both located within their fellowship and their common prayer, their worship.

And this makes complete sense, given the significance of Jesus' encounter with the two on the road to Emmaus. Christ Jesus was and is present to the church and to each Christian through the Word—the Scriptures, the apostles' teaching—read, proclaimed, studied, and obeyed.

And Christ Jesus is present to the church in a Holy Meal, the Lord's Table. The language of "devoted" suggested these were defining actions or commitments. They were the practices that made the church the church.

Evangelical Christians read all of this and they have come to the conclusion that the church is a community of the Word. And you can without doubt make this case reading Luke–Acts. Jesus was the quintessential preacher: he came on the scene as a preacher, opening the ancient Hebrew texts and proclaiming the Word. Luke 5 opens with the crowds pressing in to hear Jesus, who spoke the word of God (Lk 5:1). He taught in the synagogues (Lk 13:10); he taught from two fishing boats (Lk 5:3). He taught in the valley—Luke's counterpart to the Sermon on the Mount. And when he set his face toward Jerusalem, we read, he went through the towns and villages teaching as he made his way to the city (Lk 13:22). Jesus was a teacher.

And then when we come to the book of Acts, we can easily see how the remarkable movement and growth of the early church was carried by the preaching of the apostles.

A case could easily be made that what carries the narrative of the book of Acts is apostolic preaching. It begins with Peter on the day of Pentecost to the conclusion at the end of Acts 28 where Paul is described as "proclaiming the kingdom of God and teaching about the Lord Jesus Christ" (Acts 28:31). When a season of the life of the early church is summarized, it is captured by the line "the word of God continued to spread" (Acts 6:7) and with this, a report that the number of disciples increased significantly.

Sacramental Christians conclude that the church is fundamentally a Eucharistic community. Without discounting the importance of Scriptures and preaching, they observe that the most crucial event leading up to the Cross was the Last Supper. Jesus, we read, was eagerly looking forward to this event (Lk 22:15): he broke bread with them and then shared the cup with the phenomenal words, "This is my body, which is given for you. Do this in remembrance of me"

(Lk 22:19). And then, "This cup that is poured out for you is the new covenant in my blood" (Lk 22:20).

The bread, the cup. And this meal, as we see in Luke 24, becomes then the means by which the ascended Christ meets his church, sustains his church, and empowers the church. And what becomes clear in the book of Acts is that the church is a community that eats together. Meals play not an incidental role in the experience of faith of those who are coming to faith and those who together are seeking to live the faith.

The book of Acts actually opens with a reference to a meal; we read that Jesus was at Table with them when he told his disciples not to leave Jerusalem but to wait for the promise of the baptism of the Spirit. Then moving into the Acts narrative, early on at least, it would seem that they were meeting daily for "the breaking of bread," Luke's way of speaking of the Lord's Supper (see Acts 2:42, 46). Toward the end of the book of Acts, the practice seems to shift to weekly, as suggested by the phrase in Acts 20:7 that they "met to break bread" on the first day of the week. Regardless of whether there is an actual transition from daily worship to weekly worship, their worship, their gathering, is defined or spoken of as a meeting to break bread. In other words, for those from a sacramental perspective, that is what it means to gather: we meet at Table. It is the Table that brings the church together.

One of the most fascinating meals is that described in Acts 27, where, facing shipwreck and the potential loss of life for the entire crew on the ship taking them to Rome, Paul urges his fellow travelers to be of good cheer. And more precisely, he encouraged them through a meal. The text reads that "he took bread" and gave thanks to God, broke the bread, and urged them all to eat (Acts 27:35).

When we speak of the sacramental life of the church, we recognize that baptism is also a rather critical element in the life of the church in the book of Acts. For sacramental Christians, the church is clearly a gathering of the baptized. Virtually every reference to conversion in the book of Acts references baptism as a matter of course, as something integral to faith in Christ.

But for both the evangelical with the emphasis on the Word or the sacramental Christian with the emphasis on both baptism and the holy meal, the crucial thing to remember is that we do not speak of either the Word or the sacrament in isolation—either in isolation from each other or in isolation from the ministry of the Spirit. And most crucially, the pivotal and most central point of reference is the ascension.

Our ultimate longing is not to know the Word, but the one who is revealed to us through the Word, the risen Lord. Then also, at the meal, the meal is not an end in itself but a means by which we enter into fellowship with the risen and ascended Christ, who is the host at the meal. And our experience of the Sprit is not, ultimately, about an encounter with the Spirit. Rather the Spirit is the one by whom and through whom we live in dynamic union with Christ Jesus.

CONCLUSION

So we come back to the question. Is the church a "fellowship of the Word," or is it a Eucharistic fellowship, gathering at Table, or is the church a fellowship of the Spirit? What in the end makes the church the church? What defines the church as truly the body of Christ, growing and maturing in the grace of God, empowered and sustained for witness and mission in the world?

Could it be that the very genius of the church is that it is all three and necessarily all three? The church is a community that lives with the same immediacy of the Spirit as that witnessed to in the experience of Jesus and the early church; the church is a community of the Word, devoted to the apostolic teaching; and the church is a community of the Table, the gathering of the baptized, who, when they gather, "break bread" together.

We would be remiss to assert the importance of the evangelical, sacramental, and pentecostal character of the church without recognizing that practiced together, these elements produce further evidence that the community of faith has encountered Christ. Though it is definitely only part of the response, the experience and expression of joy typifies true connection to the Spirit in the Luke–Acts narrative.

Joy is clearly important to the Luke–Acts author. Zechariah is assured of joy to come at the birth of his son, who will be filled with the Spirit (Lk 1:14, 58). The in utero baby, John, leaps for joy in his Elizabeth's womb (Lk 1:41-44) as, we read, his mother is filled with the Spirit. And Mary's response to all of this is a song of joy, the Magnificat (Lk 1:46-55).

And then, as noted already, when the emotional life of Jesus is mentioned in Luke, he is spoken of as one who "rejoiced in the Holy Spirit" as he celebrated the joy of the seventy who returned speaking of the fruitfulness of their apostolic ministry (Lk 10:17-21).

Finally, of course, the early Christian community experienced many challenges, but it could easily be said that what marked the church was a pervasive and resilient joy. They broke bread, we read, with gladness (Acts 2:46).

Later on, when Paul would speak of his initial visit to the Thessalonian believers, he stressed that indeed the Word had come to them with power and conviction and with the Holy Spirit and that indeed they had "received the word with joy inspired by the Holy Spirit" (1 Thess 1:6).

And then, of course, we see the close link between joy and the Spirit in Acts 13:52: "The disciples were filled with joy and with the Holy Spirit."

Joy is not an incidental byproduct of what it means to be evangelical, sacramental, and pentecostal. Rather, joy is perhaps the very crucial, essential, and elemental evidence that indeed the church is living in dynamic communion with the living and ascended Christ.

THREE

THE GRACE OF GOD

Evangelical, Sacramental, and Pentecostal

IF THE CHURCH IS TO LIVE in dynamic communion with the ascended Christ and know the transforming grace of Christ, who is redeeming all things and who calls us to maturity, indeed to sainthood, we need every possible angle available to us by which we appropriate this grace.

Evangelical. Must we not be people of the Word read, preached, taught, and lived? The church, to be the church, must live by the Word of God; to be truly the church is to be a community immersed in the sacred text. To be a Christian is to live in the text and learn how ancient and sacred texts—the Hebrew Scriptures and then the writings of the apostles—are remarkably alive and current, the very lifeblood of the people of God. In worship, the Scriptures are read carefully and attentively. Ideally, this happens not merely with a verse or two projected on a screen, but first with a reading from the Hebrew Scriptures, then a reading from an Epistle, then a Gospel reading, and in there certainly a reading from the Psalms. And preaching is nothing less than the careful exposition of a text, making plain the meaning of the text so that it is understood, but more, so that those who hear grow in faith, hope, and love. It may be more than this; but it is never less than this "making plain" the ancient text.

Sacramental. Must we not be a people who take seriously the clear biblical call to the sacramental life, recognizing that baptism is the necessary and therefore indispensable counterpart to interior faith, and that the Lord's Supper is an indispensable counterpart to the preaching of the Word? We must see that faith by its very nature must be grounded—embodied through water baptism—and that we must not pit the interior call to faith against the rites which Christ himself commanded. In the sacred meal, we actually meet Christ in real time; we, in the exquisite words of the Book of Common Prayer, feed on him in our hearts by faith. This is a memorial, to be sure, but it is so much more than a memorial: it is communion; it is the bread of heaven and the cup of salvation. It is the meal without which the church cannot live. Thus if we are sacramental, it will mean, at the very least, that conversion to Christian faith necessarily includes baptism. And it will mean that as a rule, when the church gathers for worship, we will gather at the Table.

Pentecostal. And must we not be pentecostal, a people with a full-orbed—not a truncated, but a full-orbed—and dynamic theology of the Spirit? In other words, we live with a sensible awareness of the Spirit in our lives. The awareness of the Spirit and the Spirit's power infuses our individual lives. But more, we know that to be the church we need to live in the fullness of the Spirit who, in the words of the Nicene Creed, is "the Lord, the Giver of Life." New believers are incorporated into the faith through a rite of anointing with the fulsome request that they would know the filling of the Spirit. And it is sensible, meaning a felt awareness, wherein it can be said, as the apostle puts it in Romans 8, that the Spirit witnesses with our spirits that we are children of God (Rom 8:16) and in Romans 5, that in times of tribulation we do not despair, for hope does not disappoint us as the love of God is poured into our hearts by the Spirit (Rom 5:5). And the church—in worship and in mission—lives by a real-time responsiveness to the Spirit: walking in the Spirit, led by the Spirit, guided by the Spirit (Gal 5:16-25).

QUESTIONS AND OBSERVATIONS

The invitation or call to be all three—evangelical, sacramental, and pentecostal—typically raises a number of questions. Do we need to be all three? We are getting along just fine, thank you, so why make this leap, this stretch? Why insist on all three?

In response, we can of course agree that the church has indeed survived and perhaps more than just survived, actually grown and had an effective witness in the world. But still, surely we need to stress the following. First and foremost, each of these is the call of Christ. And we cannot be selective; it is not for us to choose as though we have a menu in front of us.

Second, for the church in the West, in an increasingly secular society, or where the church is a minority presence in a community or a society—whether that society be Muslim, Hindu, Buddhist, or secular, whether we are seeking to be the church in Cairo or Vancouver, wherever the church is culturally swimming upstream—surely we need every ounce of grace (if grace comes in ounces!) that might be available to us.

Christian Wiman puts it well in his book *My Bright Abyss* when he writes, "To experience grace is one thing; to integrate it into your life is quite another." We can experience the grace of God; but we surely seek to know that the full effects of the cross and the ascension— the full benefits of God's transforming grace—are fully effective in our lives, integrated, bred in the bone, and infusing our beings in such a manner that grace heals, restores, and empowers.

Why would we not devote ourselves to the oral reading of Scripture, to proclamation and teaching in our worship, as Timothy is exhorted to do (1 Tim 4:13)? This includes the public reading of Scripture, and preaching and teaching the Scriptures, as activities integral to worship and congregational life.

And why would we not baptize each new believer or not recognize that baptism is integral to authentic Christian experience? And why would we not gather at the Table each time we meet together as was the practice of the early church? Surely we would recognize that an unbaptized Christian is, if not an oxymoron, at least highly anomalous and that a worship service without the Lord's Supper is one-dimensional—not quite a full-orbed encounter with the risen and ascended Christ. Something is missing.

And why would we not ardently seek the Spirit and open our hearts and lives to an immediate encounter with the Third Person of the Trinity, who draws us into communion with Christ and with one another? Why not encourage each Christian to develop the capacity to live in and bear the fruit of the Spirit?

In other words, all three are vital and essential to the life of the church and to the growth in grace for the Christian believer. Thus I ask, why could a congregation not recognize that it behooves us, as a Christian community, to provide the means of grace to each person who affiliates with this gathering of the people of God? That the deep longing of each human soul is to know God, intimately and powerfully, and that as such, to be the church to them, we need to be all that God offers them?

When I think of individuals who live thoroughly stressed lives—at home, at work, in their physical health, and in the social dynamics of their lives, I can easily conclude that what they so urgently need is to know the grace of God. We can say, "God's grace is sufficient." But it borders on irresponsible if we do not then follow up and actually provide the *means* by which they can engage that grace, appropriate that grace, and know what it means, as Wiman puts it, that that grace is integrated into their lives.

Why would we not view it as imperative that as a congregation we are thoroughly evangelical, and unapologetically sacramental, and pentecostal?

What is the relationship between the three dimensions of divine grace? In response to this question, it is important to stress—again— that they are not each of the same type. The grace of God in the Spirit is the grace that is found in God's very self. The Spirit is very God of very God. Word and sacrament, on the other hand, are means of grace. This is an important distinction. But with that in mind, consider the following.

The pentecostal, so taken with the immediate awareness of the Spirit, needs to appreciate that Word and sacrament are the God-given means by which the Spirit's ministry is anchored and communicated to the church. It is Word and sacrament that establish the Spirit's ministry as precisely the ministry of the risen Christ. Without Word and sacrament, our experience of the Spirit easily descends into sentimentality and self-indulgence.

The evangelical, so taken with the power of the Word and the call to faith—trusting faith in the Word—would appreciate that faith must be embodied, grounded, to truly take effect. Without this sacramental embodiment we so easily confuse faith with cerebral acknowledgement, belief with (mere) understanding. But more, we need to affirm that without the immediate witness of the Spirit in our reading, study, and preaching, Scripture is nothing but words on a page, ink on paper. When the Scriptures are preached, they certainly do illumine the mind, rekindle the heart, and strengthen the will. But the Scriptures only empower and equip in the power of the Spirit. Thus we always read and preach with attentiveness to the Spirit and a deliberate humble dependence on the Spirit. There is indeed a pentecostal hermeneutic that would inform the evangelical reading of Scripture. And more, the sacramental tradition would help the evangelical interpret the Scriptures within and as part of the living tradition of the church.

And the sacramental Christian would, of course, recognize that what gives meaning or content to baptism and the Lord's Supper is the Word preached; that we come to the waters of baptism and to the Holy Meal with hearts and minds that have been attentive and responsive to the Word; that the Word, properly speaking, always precedes the sacramental rite, necessarily so, for the rite in itself is just a rite. It is so easily an empty rite if it is not informed—even more, informed and then infused—with the power of the God who created all things by speaking. But more, we must stress that both baptism and the Lord's Supper are supremely pentecostal acts, acts of the Spirit. Christ is truly and fully present in the celebration of the Lord's Supper, but it is a presence that is effected through the Holy Spirit. Thus we must insist on the *epiclēsis*—the prayer for the coming, anointing, and empowerment of the Holy Spirit—when we participate in the celebration of this sacred meal. A fuller exploration of this idea appears in chapter five, "The Sacramental Principle."

John Calvin observes that the "sacraments fulfill their office only when the Spirit, that inward teacher, comes to them, by whose power alone hearts are penetrated and affections moved and our souls opened for the sacraments to enter in. If the Spirit be lacking, the sacraments can accomplish nothing more in our minds than the splendor of the sun shining upon blind eyes or a voice sounding in deaf ears."

What of Christ? Then also, we must come back to this question: Where is Christ himself in all of this? Ultimately our focus, our attention is not on the Word or the sacrament, or even on the Spirit, but on Christ. The genius of the ecology of grace is that each is a means—not alone, but in tandem—by which Christ is known. And yet the danger of disconnection from our living head, Christ Jesus, still remains.

The Word, when it is an end in itself and not (merely) a means by which Christ is revealed and known, is, well, deadly. Biblicism does not animate or sustain the life of the church. The Bible is the Word of God, of course, but only insofar as in and through the Word we are drawn into fellowship with Christ. We ultimately do not long to know the Word, but to know Christ. When the Word is preached, we long to know, love, and serve Jesus.

In the celebration of the sacraments, we do not confuse the symbol with the reality. While it is true that to participate in the symbol is to participate in what the symbol symbolizes, we still must not confuse the symbol with the reality, nor ascribe to the symbol—the bread/cup—the honor that is ultimately only due to Christ himself. The sacrament is a means by which we know Christ; it is a means, not an end.

Even regarding the Spirit, we long, ultimately, not for an encounter with the Spirit but an encounter with Christ. We long for the Spirit's presence and power in our life that we might be "in Christ." Further, the determinative evidence that the Spirit is among us, that the Spirit is at work in our midst, is not extraordinary manifestations, even healings, however wonderful these might be. Rather, the evidence that the Spirit is present among us is that Christ is glorified, that women and men choose to know, love, and serve Christ Jesus.

Each of these—the evangelical, the sacramental, and the pentecostal—is almost deadly when not linked intimately to Christ Jesus himself (or when confused with Christ). The ecology of grace is ultimately about knowing, loving, and serving Christ Jesus; it is finally about union with Christ and participation in the life of Christ. Arising from and leading to the experience of Christ, in union with

Christ, these three means of grace are a tremendous provision by God—of God's very self in the person of the Holy Spirit, and then the remarkable gifts of Word and sacrament—and when in dynamic connection, when taken together, they have the potential to be a means by which the church and the world know the transforming grace of God. Together they are the ecology of grace.

JOHN CALVIN AND THE ECOLOGY OF GRACE

Many within the evangelical theological and spiritual tradition might wonder if this overview of the ecology of grace is truly consistent with their own evangelical heritage. Naturally, the bottom line is not whether this particular tradition is right, but whether, in the end, it is truly the design and intent of God for the Christian and for the church. And yet it is worth asking the question: How would the forerunners of the evangelical tradition approach the question of the ecology of grace?

Here it helps to appeal again to the great Protestant Reformer, John Calvin, who speaks powerfully to the vital place of each in the life of the Christian in his magisterial *Institutes of the Christian Religion.*

Regarding the Word. While Calvin had a profound regard for the Christian theological tradition and the witness of the church fathers, he insisted on the primacy of Scripture in the development of Christian thought and practice. The Scriptures were, for him, the supreme means by which God is known or revealed. While fully acknowledging the power and potential of what theologians have typically spoken of as "general revelation"—God's self-revelation through the created order—for Calvin there is simply no substitute for the written, inscripturated Word of God, which provides the church with divine wisdom. Scripture is the guide to doctrine and the guide to the life of the church.

Regarding the sacraments. John Calvin was also remarkably sacramental in his theological sensibilities. Many of his heirs within the Reformed theological tradition and many evangelical and pentecostal Christians who would recognize Calvin as one of the architects of the Protestant Reformation view these as secondary and almost incidental to the Christian life. One gets the impression from many evangelical and pentecostal Christians, including many who would self-identify as Calvinist and Reformed, that it is possible to have a full-orbed Christian life with minimal exposure to the sacraments. They insist that baptism and the Lord's Supper are not in themselves means of grace and that this conviction is somehow consistent with the spiritual heritage and tradition of the Protestant Reformation. Many Christians assume that the perspective on the sacraments of Ulrich Zwingli—that the rites of baptism and the Lord's Supper are mere tokens, at best, and certainly not a means of grace—is the de facto perspective of evangelical Protestants, and thus that anyone who is "sacramental" is more Catholic than Protestant.

To the contrary, the other Reformers were all more appreciative of the role of the sacraments in the life of the church, not least John Calvin, who was profoundly sacramental in his understanding of the church and the Christian life. While Augustine was the first to give the technical definition of a sacrament as a sign, "a visible sign of invisible grace," it is Calvin who writes that a sacrament is "an external sign, by which the Lord seals on our conscience his promises of good-will toward us, in order to sustain the weakness of our faith."

While Calvin rejected transubstantiation, he nevertheless insisted that that body of Christ is present in the celebration of the Lord's Supper and that the bread, while always remaining bread, is the very means by which Christ is fully present to his people through the ministry of the Holy Spirit. And as such, the Table is an indispensable means by which the Christian community experiences the grace of God—regularly, as an integral dimension of Christian worship.

Regarding the Spirit. Calvin makes this observation at the beginning of Book III of the Institutes:

> First, we must understand that as long as Christ remains outside of us, and we are separated from him, all that he has suffered and done for the salvation of the human race remains useless and of no value for us . . . all that he possesses is nothing to us until we grow into one body with him. It is true that we obtain this by faith. Yet since we see that not all indiscriminately embrace the communion with Christ which is offered through the gospel, reason itself teaches us to climb higher and to examine into the secret energy of the Spirit, by which we come to enjoy Christ and all his benefits.

As I will note in the upcoming chapter on the pentecostal tradition, Calvin was resistant to the suggestion that there might be a direct witness of the Spirit, an experience of the Spirit unmediated by the Scriptures or the Sacraments. And in sixteenth century context, given the continued threat within the church from those who disregarded the objective witness of the Spirit in the Scriptures, this response may be understandable. But what should not be missed is that Calvin had a richly nuanced theology of the Spirit, recognizing that—and this is crucial—the Scriptures have no power or grace in themselves, but only insofar as the Spirit is active and dynamically present in the Word as it is read, preached, and lived. For Calvin, it was by Word and Spirit that the church knows the grace of God.

JOHN WESLEY'S WITNESS TO THE THREE-FOLD ECOLOGY OF GRACE

In speaking of the ecology of grace as pentecostal, evangelical, and sacramental, many would naturally recognize that there are those in the history of the church who are exemplars of this three-fold vision. Surely one of these is John Wesley, the founder of Methodism and a key figure in the rise of Evangelicalism in the 18th century. We could do a comprehensive review of Wesley's work, but for my purposes here it is sufficient to reference his sermons—particularly those that reflect some of his key convictions about the life and witness of the church.

His pentecostal (small *p*) vision is evident in two sermons: "The Witness of the Spirit 1," and the "The Witness of the Spirit 2." The essence of the pentecostal principle is found here: the Spirit's presence and ministry in the life of the Christian and the life of the church is immediate, or put differently, unmediated. There was without doubt a pentecostal thread or movement within the Christian church throughout her entire history; but when we think of the emergence of the pentecostal movement in the twentieth century, virtually any historical analysis will take us back to the experience of Wesley at Aldersgate and with this the articulation of a particular understanding of the ministry of the Spirit.

The essence of his experience and thus of his message, in this regard, was the possibility—and more, the indispensability—of an immediate experience of the grace of God effected in our lives by the Holy Spirit. The Spirit witnesses with our spirits that we are children of God (Rom 8:16). It is immediate, it is effective, and its fruits are evident in the character of our lives and in the abiding joy by which we live in a fragmented world.

Second, when it comes to the evangelical principle, there are many sermons to which I could turn. Perhaps most notable is the fact that Wesley spoke of himself as *homo unius libri*, "a man of one book," and he spoke in a similar vein about the early Methodists as "Bible-Christians," who when gathered, would preach "plain, old Bible-Christianity."

It is important to stress something at this point. It is often said that the Wesley theological tradition is marked by what is typically spoken of as a quadrilateral and that the source of Wesleyan theology is fourfold: Scripture, tradition, reason, and experience. This is a helpful way to speak of this particular religious movement, but only to a point. Wesley was without doubt one who affirmed the significance of experience as a source for theological reflection and theology. And he certainly affirmed the weight of the Christian creedal tradition. And he was one to affirm that the God-given capacity for rational thought needed to be a significant and critical point of reference in doing theology. Thus some have actually criticized Wesley as not truly evangelical because Scripture was not his only source for theology. Yet his own testimony, as noted above, and his practice suggest that he was evangelical in this: the lifeblood of his preaching was Scripture. Scott Jones examines the way in which Wesley actually uses Scripture, noting the following:

The authority Wesley grants to the Scripture as divinely inspired writings, almost downplaying their human character;

Thus, of course, because they are divine in origin, the Scriptures are true, trustworthy and infallible;

As such, Scripture is the sole authority when it comes to Christian doctrine and practice; and, finally;

Scripture is to be read and interpreted as a whole, as a unified testimony to the saving work of God.

In other words, those from an evangelical theological and spiritual tradition would naturally recognize that these are precisely the sensibilities, with regard to Scripture, of an evangelical Christian.

And last, Wesley was actually more sacramental that most of his followers. I think of what for many of us is a favorite of Wesley's sermons, his delightful "The Duty of Constant Communion" (Sermon 101), where he urges his readers to be present frequently for the Lord's Supper, daily if not weekly, but at the very least weekly. This sermon reflects something at the heart of Wesley's understanding of the church and of the Christian life. Most Evangelicals who read Wesley either skip over his sacramental vision or they just chalk it up to an inconsistency in his theology. But Wesley is unavoidably a theologian and churchman who stands within the breadth of the catholic and thus sacramental life of the church. For Wesley, baptism is an essential part of the initiation into Christian faith, into life in Christ, and into Christian community. He does not speak of baptism at the expense of faith; he does not pit the interior experience of faith and repentance as over against baptism. He does not speak of the inner life of faith and repentance and with this the experience of the regenerating work of God as though this can happen apart from the sacramental life of the church. While a case can certainly be made that Wesley prioritizes the interior experience, we are not truly Wesleyan until and unless we recognize the significance of baptism and the Lord's Supper in his vision of the church and of the spiritual life.

Some have insisted that in seeking to affirm all three—the inner witness, the priority of the Scriptures, and the vital necessity of the sacrament—Wesley had an inconsistent theological vision. And it has been a challenge for Wesley scholars to find coherence. How did Wesley do it? How did he manage to believe in the inner witness, the pentecostal impulse, together with his deep commitment to the Scriptures in his own life and the life of the church, along with the sacramentalism that he inherited from his Anglican heritage? Can Wesley live out his Anglican sacramental sensibilities along with his evangelical commitment to Scripture and his appreciation of the immediacy—a pentecostal immediacy of the Spirit in personal religious experience? Can Wesley truly be an Evangelical with his emphasis on the sacraments?

While Wesley was not a systematic theologian and thus perhaps did not to our contemporary satisfaction provide his readers with clarity on this point, there is no doubt that for Wesley, regardless of all other variables, religious experience was personal and heartfelt. The transforming dynamic for Wesley is the renewal of the heart. And it is my take and that of others that this perspective provides coherence to the Wesleyan vision of the Christian life. Clearly this inner transformation of the heart is unequivocally the work of the Spirit. Religious experience is personal and subjective. It was and is transformative, precisely because it is the fruit of the Spirit within us. But the work of the Spirit is always grounded in and accompanied by the ministry of the Word. And the interior reality—in the great tradition of the sacramentalism from St. Augustine onwards—is necessarily expressed and embodied in the sacramental life of the church. Pentecostals like Wesley; he talks their kind of language when it comes to the Spirit. Evangelicals like to hear him say that he is a man of one book. And Anglicans read him and say, "He's one of us!" All of them, reading Wesley, will inevitably come back to the heart "strangely warmed." And yet when they do, they find someone who affirmed the pentecostal, evangelical, and sacramental dimensions of the ecology of God's grace in the life of the Christian and in the life of the church.

CONCLUSION

I reference John Calvin's *Institutes* and make this more extended commentary on John Wesley out of the following conviction: in my circles, evangelical Christians typically assume that it is not consistent with the evangelical theological and spiritual tradition to affirm the sacraments and to profile the immediacy of the Spirit in the life of the church and the life of the Christian.

What I hope is clear is that the call to be evangelical, sacramental, and pentecostal is not a threat to one's evangelical theological and spiritual sensibilities. Those within sacramental and pentecostal traditions could perhaps do this same exercise from their perspective. Thus I suggest that whether one comes to this question from a sacramental, evangelical, or pentecostal heritage and perspective, the bottom line remains: the biblical witness and the historic witness of the church consistently call the church to a fully orbed embracing of the vital means by which the grace of the risen and ascended Christ is made present in the life of the church.

FOUR

THE EVANGELICAL PRINCIPLE

IT MAY BE A CARICATURE, but there is truth in the observation that nothing quite defines Evangelicals as well as that they are "Bible-believing Christians." Few if any Evangelicals would resist this observation; most would actually signal this as a point of pride. Some Evangelicals might insist that this is one-sided, and of course it is. And yet for many years the Evangelical Theological Society only had one criteria for membership, that one affirmed the inerrancy of Scripture. Many an ETS session has been spent debating the "real" meaning of *inerrancy*, and life would be grim for any member whose understanding of inerrancy did not quite pass muster.

Evangelicals typically affirm that all theological and ethical debates are resolved, quite simply, by an appeal to the authoritative text, the Bible. And they get distressed and might even question the legitimacy of any Christian group or movement that did not appeal to the Scriptures as the final authority—not as an authority, but as the one and *only* authority in the life of the church.

Those of more sacramental traditions and those of more pentecostal and often of more Wesleyan traditions often struggle to comprehend this seeming obsession with how the authority of Scripture is defined. But there is something in this focus on the Biblical text that merits the consideration of all Christians. When this attention to the text neglects the immediate work of the Spirit, so that the redeeming work of God is not appreciated as through Word *and* Spirit, and when this emphasis on the Scriptures discounts the sacramental and creedal heritage of the church, there is a problem—a big problem. And yet we must not miss the way in which the evangelical heritage consistently affirms and keeps the broader church attentive to a vital principle I am here speaking of as the "evangelical principle," the principle that affirms and consistently stresses that the Scriptures play an animating role in the life of the church, not in a secondary sense, but as a primary means by which God is present to the church and a primary means by which the church appropriates and lives in the grace of the risen and ascended Christ. Christ Jesus is present to and with the church through the Word and graces the church through the sacred text. The church is a community that is appropriately described as the "fellowship of the Word."

What does "fellowship of the Word" mean in actual practice? What would the Evangelical say to those of more sacramental and charismatic or pentecostal perspectives on why the Word is animating—a means of grace? I suggest that, from an evangelical perspective, knowing the grace of God through the Word is evident in two things:

1. Evangelicals seek dynamic theology of the Word, indicating how the Scriptures are organically linked with the creative and redemptive power of God, indicating how the Scriptures function as the Word of God.

2. Evangelicals consider the fundamental practices by which the individual Christian and the faith community might engage the Scriptures and know the Scriptures as a means of grace.

Nevertheless, Evangelicals need to listen and respond to the critique that comes from those who view them through the lens of the sacramental and pentecostal perspectives. Therefore, this chapter will proceed to further develop the above two evangelical contributions to the understanding of the ecology of grace and then explore a vital critique or caution.

THE THEOLOGY OF THE WORD: THE SEQUENCE OF CREATION, LOGOS, THE APOSTLES, AND SCRIPTURE

It is essential, absolutely essential, that our understanding of the Scripture and the place of the Scriptures in the life of the church and as a means of grace be located within a comprehensive understanding of the Word of God.

We begin by the telling observation that the whole of creation comes into being through and by the Word of God; God spoke, and created order came into being. And God declared that it is good. Genesis 1 testifies to this powerfully, with the recurring line "And God said" and its counterpart, "And God saw that it was good."

Many debates about the meaning of Genesis 1, including questions of the significance of the days and how literally we are to take them, completely miss the main point of Genesis 1: all things have come into being through the power of a God who speaks, and who in speaking acts, and whose actions, when complete, are good.

The affirmation of the creative Word of God is then complemented by the stunning affirmation of the Christian theological tradition that the Word of God finds particular expression through the second person of the Holy Trinity, the Son, who is the Word but then becomes the Word incarnate.

We would be hard-pressed to have a theology of the Word without reference to the opening words of the Gospel of John and the Letter to the Hebrews. The dramatic turning point in the history of the world comes precisely at that point where now God has spoken very specifically through the Son (Heb 1:2). To this the phenomenal opening of the Gospel of John also testifies: "In the beginning was the Word, and the Word was with God, and the Word was God" (Jn 1:1).

And it is this Word that then becomes flesh (Jn 1:14) and comes to the world as the very embodiment of God, more specifically, as the Word of God. And it is as the incarnate Word that the glory of God is revealed.

We then see Jesus, the incarnate Word, as quintessentially a teacher. The grace of God is known through the person of Christ Jesus; but we must not miss that the revelation of God in Christ comes through the one who is first and foremost one who teaches. Jesus is a rabbi; he has followers; he teaches them. They are his disciples specifically because they attend to his teaching. He taught in larger settings, with as many as five thousand attending to his words, and he taught in intimate settings, whether the mid-night visit of Nicodemus or the mid-day encounter with the woman at the well. He taught his disciples in parables and in extended expositions. He taught in more structured settings, including the synagogue, and in more informal contexts. When an occasion arose, Jesus seized the moment to speak to the meaning of the kingdom. He taught by example, of course (consider the washing of the disciples' feet, Jn 13:1-5), but the life of Jesus would not have its power and meaning in the life of the church were it not for the words Jesus spoke that interpreted his actions and located them in the broader purposes of God.

And this is the pivotal piece: when Jesus speaks, salvation comes. The one through whom all things were created through speaking (Jn 1:1) is now the one through whom all things are redeemed and made whole—again, through speaking. The same power that brought into being the cosmos is the power by which the cosmos will be saved.

And this is the power of God now in Christ who speaks and stills the wind and the waves (Mk 4:35-41), the one who in speaking has the words of eternal life. God has spoken by a Son (Heb 1:2), and "he sustains all things by his powerful word" (Heb 1:3).

Jesus certainly performed wonderful acts—as healer, but more, in the specific work of sacrificial service, though the cross and through the movements of God from cross, to resurrection to ascension to the sending of the Spirit. And we look forward to the day when in Christ, all will be made well at the consummation of the kingdom. But what carries this narrative is the Word spoken—proclamation, preaching, teaching. And it is to this Word that the church attends, for this Word is grace, the very grace of God. In God's speaking in Christ, God acts; the spoken Word brings about the salvation of God.

Another dimension of the Word of God is that it finds expression through the spokespersons for God, the prophets and the apostles. The deep assumption and remarkable witness found in the Scriptures is that persons—designated prophets and apostles—were the instruments or means by which God spoke. Interestingly enough, we have no direct words from Jesus, the Son of God, the Word incarnate, red letter versions of the Bible notwithstanding. Rather, literally all of God's speaking is through the prophets and the apostles. The only testimony we have from God is mediated to the church through the witness of those appointed to speak for God. God spoke by the prophets. And Jesus commissioned apostles to be the spokespersons for his gospel. The Hebrew Scriptures—the Older Testament—are the witness, the words, the speaking, of the prophets. And we read that the early church "devoted themselves" to the apostles teaching (Acts 2:42), recognizing the continuity with the prophets and leaning into their witness, the witness of the apostles, as specifically the continuing Word of God. Thus we have the wonderful turn of phrase, or image, in Ephesians 2:20: the church is built on the foundation of the apostles and prophets, with Christ Jesus himself as the cornerstone of this "structure."

What this speaks to is the remarkably human character of the Word of God—that God has chosen to be present to the world and thus to the church through the words, the speaking, of ordinary mortals. But more, it means very simply this: we do not know the grace of God until and unless we attend to the words—the very words—of those who have been commissioned by God to speak for God: the prophets and the apostles. There is no bypassing these voices. To the contrary: the church thrives and the salvation of God is known if and as we learn to lean into the witness of these spokespersons for God. When they speak, God speaks through them and by them. Their words are the Word of God.

And the church has always recognized that the Scriptures—Old and New Testament—represent this prophetic and apostolic witness. And the church has always affirmed that, to use specific and precise language, "the canon is closed." This is it; we do not have more books or chapters to add to this witness.

And yet while affirming that the Scriptures are indeed a human word—the words of the prophets and the apostles—in the end, when the church gathers for worship, the Scriptures, the sacred text, are, when all is said and done, the Word of God.

The witness of the apostles and the prophets is the witness of God—the revelation of the Triune God that is not merely information *about* God, but the communication of God's very self. And it is this precise quality to the Scriptures that makes the Bible so compelling, that so captures the evangelical imagination. The unique relationship with God—that the Bible is "God's Word"—is what makes the Scriptures the text of, and for, the church. And more, from this point of departure we must speak of the connection between the Bible and the grace of God. The Christian community is created, formed and re-formed by the Scriptures. While speaking of the Scriptures as the Word of the Triune God is appropriate, when we speak of the grace of God, we speak of the grace of God communicated to the church and to the world through the ascended Christ. The Scriptures properly speaking, then, are the Word of God insofar as they are the word of Christ. When the church gathers for worship and the Scriptures are opened, read, and preached, the church is attentive, eagerly attentive, for this simple yet extraordinary reason: when the Scriptures are proclaimed, Christ is proclaimed. Even more, Christ is doing the proclaiming.

And thus, we must speak of preaching as also "the Word of God." The evangelical theological and spiritual tradition, as heirs to the Protestant Reformation, has viewed itself as the Christian movement that moved the pulpit front and center—visually representing that when the church gathers for worship, the centerpiece of worship is that moment when the Scriptures are open and read and then, and this is the crucial piece, the Scriptures are proclaimed or preached. This too is the Word of God; this too is God speaking.

And yet the evangelical tradition has also always insisted that preaching is only the Word of God insofar it is faithful to the apostolic witness, when it is nothing more than making plain the meaning of the ancient text and what that ancient text might mean for the church today (see Paul's language to describe his own preaching in 2 Cor 4:2). Sure, we can be creative and, of course, the preacher makes the connection to the contemporary social, economic, and political context. But—and this is crucial—the genius of preaching is precisely that the ancient Word is made present. Not just an ancient idea, but the sacred text read, opened, made clear and plain and accessible.

Preaching and the Scriptures themselves are the Word of God, but only as a means to an end; they exist so the church would know

Christ Jesus, who is the Incarnate Word. The Scriptures are the means by which Christ is known. Even though as a worshiper in the pew, I long for the preacher to be faithful to the ancient text, in the end it is not the Bible I long to know but Jesus. The genius of great preaching is not that the biblical text is known through careful exegesis but that God in Christ is revealed.

And yet the point here is that this cannot happen unless we are careful with our exegesis. It is not either/or. We come to the Scriptures that we might know Christ; but we cannot assume or hope to know Christ until and unless we are faithful to the Scriptures.

Having stressed the connection between the Scriptures and the grace of God in Christ, it is also important that we consider the actual character of the biblical text that has been received. Two things must be stressed that have a profound bearing on how the Scriptures are read and preached. First, the Bible is a single document. However much we make of each the sixty-six books, their distinctive character, and the variety of genres, in the end, this is the God-story, the narrative of God's self-revelation through the actions of God as Creator and Redeemer and the formation for God of a people. Thus each segment of Holy Scripture is and must be read in light of the whole. And, of course, the Scriptures find their canonical center in the Gospels.

Second, there is a deeply human character to the Scriptures. They are unavoidably very human documents and letters. However much the evangelical tradition affirms that the Bible is "God's Word," and appropriately so, the fact remains that these are the writings of prophets and apostles—storytellers, poets, letter-writers, sages, and dreamers. Every text of Scripture comes to the biblical canon through the pen of a human author. The humanity of the text is deeply apparent. And the critical point is that this deeply human character to the Bible does not diminish its authority or the fact that the Bible is respected and honored as being very truly "the Word." A colleague put it so well: "I think most Christians underestimate the 'human character' of the Scriptures . . . and the degree to which God accommodates himself to the contexts in which he speaks. The miracle of grace is that a profoundly 'accommodated word' can simultaneously speak to a universal truth."

This then is a crucial working principle: to know the divine character to the Bible—to know God's Word—we must attend to the very humanity of the text. We know the divine Word by attending to the human word. This means that we attend to the details. We recognize the importance of exegesis as an essential and critical practice that supports the theological formation of the Christian community. We view attending to the text given as an opportunity, not a burden; this due diligence is a critical capacity for all who take the Scriptures seriously.

Two attitudes characterize this careful attention to the Word. First, exegesis opens up the text and asks, very specifically, how is this text meant to be the action of God, the performance of God, in this community? How does God wish to speak through this text to the community that is reading and hearing this text proclaimed? And this always and consistently means that the text is heard within the broader context of the story of God. Moreover, we consider how the text is to be heard in the context of the story, the lives and situations of the people who are hearing the text read and proclaimed. Thus we hear the text as for the very first time.

A musician playing Beethoven does not alter and would not think of altering the notes of Beethoven's composition. Similarly, exegesis is an act of love, meaning both a respect for the text but also delight in the text—in the language, the words, the metaphors and ultimately the extraordinary self-revelation of God in the text. But two renderings of the same Beethoven sonata can be very different, as presented and played by the particular pianist. And in like manner, when the text is preached, it is by this preacher, in this community, for such a time as this. It always has an immediacy to it.

Second, and perhaps most fundamentally, Evangelicals take the text seriously, granting it unique authority. They read the text, attend to the text, defer to the text. If they question it, they recognize that they question it from a disposition of meekness and humility. Evangelicals would assume that we do not have the option to pick or choose which parts we like or even, in a sense, to "reframe" the text in modern terms so that it is more palatable. The Bible is not viewed as ancient or antiquated or needing to be modernized. Rather, it is viewed as stunningly relevant to contemporary life. And it is assumed that the Christian and the church can read the Scriptures as though each word, each phrase, each paragraph, and each verse are the very words of God.

THE PRACTICES:
BIBLE STUDY, PREACHING, MEDITATION

While I here speak specifically to the importance of preaching, it is important to locate preaching within other practices that the evangelical tradition has consistency profiled and encouraged. The evangelical theological and spiritual tradition has consistently stressed the defining and critical role of the Scriptures in the life of the church and the life of the Christian. The odds are, if you are a university student and you see a sign posted for an early morning Bible study, the group meeting would self-identify as Evangelicals. They are into Bible study! And evangelical publishing houses tend to put out guides to Bible study.

Evangelical seminaries emphasize—and rightly so—as vitally important that those anticipating religious leadership within faith communities need to be students of the Scriptures. That is, they need to attend to the original languages, master the skill of careful exegesis and the art of biblical interpretation, and then, in turn, allow that in-depth Bible study to inform and support their preaching.

Evangelicals would typically assume that all Christians could benefit from if not actually need sustained, focused study of the Scriptures. It would be the evangelical ideal that a Christian would be biblically literate and have the capacity to appreciate both the full scope of the biblical narrative and the unique significance of distinct literary genres in Scripture—appreciating the difference between narrative, poetry, wisdom literature, epistle, and apocalyptic literature, for example.

Evangelicals have also stressed the importance of meditation—the careful, focused, and open-hearted attention to the text of Scripture. This reading goes beyond analysis and study to attentiveness to the ways in which God is specifically speaking to this person in this time and place, an attentiveness to the text such that the language of feeding and nourishment has been used to signal that the Bible is actually the spiritual lifeblood of the Christian soul.

And this suggests something so very crucial: new Christians, as part of their initiation into the Christian faith, have, as part of that process—as an integral part of that process—a study program by which they are taught to read the Bible for themselves for spiritual profit, for spiritual growth, for understanding, and for an increased capacity for growth in wisdom.

The evangelical principle is cogently captured, therefore, by the words of 1 Peter 1:22-25, which affirms in close succession two critical perspectives. First, the means of coming to Christian faith is through the Word. Thus the line "you have been born anew . . . through the living and enduring word of God. . . . That word is the good news that was announced to you" (1 Pet 1:23-25). But then, second, it naturally follows that this Word would also be the means by which one grows and matures in faith. Therefore Peter urges those new in the faith, who are compared to "newborn infants," to seek the "milk" that would be the very nourishment for their growth (1 Pet 2:2). For those of an evangelical persuasion, Bible study is a fundamental spiritual practice in that it provides the nourishment essential for growth in faith. It is a means of grace.

This study, meditation, and serious engagement in the Scriptures is complemented and finds its fulfillment, its denouement, perhaps, in the gathering of the church where the high point in the liturgy centers around the text. Typically this follows the sequence of the reading of the sacred text, followed by the prayer for illumination, and then in the minutes to follow—ideally not too many minutes!—proclamation and exposition as the preacher considers with the congregation the ancient Word and what this sacred text might mean for the people of God today, how indeed God is present to and speaking and gracing God's people within the specific context of their cultural, social, economic, and political situation.

Evangelicals see the focus on teaching in the ministry of Jesus and the crucial role of preaching in the book of Acts. They also appreciate such references as Nehemiah 8, with his dramatic description of the Levitical priesthood opening the sacred text, reading the text, and then explaining the meaning of text, all to great joy for those who heard. The language of the apostle Paul as he speaks of his own ministry as a preacher emphasizes that his approach was not one of rhetoric or oratory, per se, but of simple dependence on the power of God, which he links to the wisdom of Christ. Paul was quite capable of rhetoric, as is evident in numerous segments of his writings, including the grand doxology found in the closing verses of Romans 8. For the Evangelical, rhetoric or oratory ultimately serve the text, or more specifically, the Word that emerges from and is proclaimed through the exposition of the ancient text. The pastoral epistles consistently emphasize the importance of preaching with a twofold emphasis on the oral reading of Scripture and the importance of sustaining the ministry of the Word "in season and out of season," resisting the temptation to become nothing more than an entertainer (2 Tim 4:2 NASB). Further, we see an urgent plea in 1 Timothy 4:13 for the oral reading of Scripture and for preaching and teaching. For the evangelical tradition, a pastor is a preacher/teacher in that the church knows the grace of God and grows in grace as it engages, knows, and comes to live in the Word.

Regarding the oral reading of Scripture. Many in the evangelical tradition have long since dispensed with the oral reading of Scripture in public worship, at most reading a brief segment or verse of Scripture here or there. The observation is often made that the ancient church needed this feature, the oral reading of Scripture, because it was the only way the average person could actually hear the text, and that the oral reading of Scripture is not so essential when copies of the Scripture are so readily available to all. This perspective misses something that all children know, even those who know how to read: few things are so powerful, dramatic, and actually transformative as a public reading, even when one and all know the text. The irony for me is this: if I want to be in worship where the Scriptures are read as a standard part of the liturgy, I need to go for worship at the more sacramental traditions—Anglican, Catholic, for example—which will typically have four readings every Sunday (Old Testament, Psalm, Epistle, Gospel). And I never tire of that oral reading; to the contrary, we can learn to attend as though for the very first time. In the oral reading as often as not, something connects—a fresh engagement with the text—even if the hearer is actually one who has read that very text many, many times.

Regarding preaching, one caveat is required. Evangelical congregations often experience Sunday preaching that is little more than good advice on this, that, or the other topic that the pastor deems to be relevant to the life of the congregation. But the evangelical tradition recognizes that at its best, preaching is not good advice but the gospel—the congregation being drawn into the grand narrative of the work of God, Creator and Redeemer, and in this encounter with the Word, one and all come to see their own lives with and informed by this narrative. Thus, ideally, each text is preached through the lens of the gospel and in light of the story of God and of God's redemptive purposes.

Of great importance, the end it is not the text that is preached but that Christ Jesus is revealed through the text. And more, it is specifically, as the apostle puts it, "Christ crucified" (1 Cor 1:23). There is indeed a canonical center to the Scriptures—especially the Gospel narratives, and more, even these Gospels finds their visceral pivot in the cross—so that all of Scripture is preached in light of the passion of Christ Jesus.

While we can unequivocally affirm the authority and trustworthiness of Scriptures, we still need to be very sure that our approach to Scripture is consistent with how the Scriptures actually function in the life of the church. Evangelicals affirm the authority of Scripture, but it is imperative that our approach to the Scriptures be consistent with how God intends the Scriptures to be used. And most central or pivotal in this regard is, as Christian Smith puts it: "The purpose, center, and interpretive key to Scripture is Jesus Christ." Quite simply, the Bible only has meaning in light of the Christ event, and we read the Scriptures as those who are in dynamic fellowship with Christ, who is Lord of the church.

WORD AND SACRAMENT, WORD AND SPIRIT

As noted, we come to two crucial caveats to our understanding of the place of the Scriptures in the life of the church. The great danger of the evangelical tradition—its Achilles heel, one might say—is that the very point of strength, the affirmation of the vital place of the Scriptures in the life of the church, would become an unfortunate weakness. If the Scriptures, along with Bible study and consistent preaching, are not seen in vital association with the sacraments, and if this affirmation of the Scriptures is not deeply linked with the ministry of the Holy Spirit, then, ironically, the church does not actually live in the fullness of the indwelling Word.

First, it is vital that the evangelical tradition hear from those of a more sacramental persuasion to appreciate the link between Word and sacrament, an essential counterpoint in the life of the church and in the experience or appropriation of the grace of the risen Christ.

The New Testament witness suggests that the sacramental actions of the church are essential—not secondary, but essential—to the capacity of the Christian community to receive the Word, specifically the Word proclaimed or preached. Thus the necessary counterpart to the initial proclamation, to evangelism, is baptism; the equally necessary counterpart to the proclaimed Word in the weekly liturgy is the Table. Word and Table. Each needs the other. The Word preached is not for a moment diminished by the engagement with the Living Word at the Table that follows; rather, the two strengthen and reinforce each other.

The Evangelical would insist that catechesis, preaching, and teaching precede baptism and give meaning to baptism. Catechesis is the religious orientation and instruction that informs our experience of baptism. Preaching and teaching invite us and empower us to live in the truth and the faith of the church into which we are being baptized.

Yet the Evangelical needs to appreciate that baptism is essential. In a very real sense, the gospel has not been truly received in the life of a person coming to faith until and unless one is baptized. I will speak more to this, of course, in chapter five, "The Sacramental Principle." Here it is sufficient to stress that the sacramental perspective does not for a moment threaten the integrity of evangelism and the preaching of the gospel but only reinforces and strengthens it.

In weekly worship, the same principle applies. The Word is heard, and then at the Table, the Word is received, consumed, embodied.

But there is more to what we might call the sacramental corrective to biblicism. Through the sacraments, the Christian enters into fellowship not merely with the ascended Christ, but with the church. The Christian is part of the sacramental community that stretches back to the apostles. This is a powerful reminder that we read the Scriptures and proclaim the Scriptures in light of the ancient creeds and in light of the church's worship of the ascended Christ. The church, or better, the faith of the church as expressed in the Creed, anchors and informs and governs the way in which the Scriptures are read. The text is never read in isolation from the church and, specifically, the church in organic fellowship with Christ.

Thus no text is read in isolation from the rest of Scripture. But more, the text is not read or preached in isolation from the church as a living community in dynamic fellowship with Christ.

When we speak of the church, for those with a sacramental perspective, the saints matter; they are living embodiments of the very message of Scripture. Or as Curtis W. Freeman put it so well, the lives of the saints are "faithful performances of Scripture"—powerful and dynamic illustrations of what it means to live in Christ and to follow Christ and be transformed into the image of Christ.

Second, the pentecostal principle gives us the language of Word and Spirit. The great gift of the Scriptures can only be received "in the Spirit."

This means, of course, that we recognize the work of the Spirit in providentially bringing to the church and giving to the church the text that we have. In this we recognize the work of the Spirit in the lives and witness of those human sources or authors through which the text of Scripture is spoken—the work of the prophets and apostles (see 2 Tim 3:16).

But then also, it is vital to affirm the work of the Spirit in the task or practice of reading the Scriptures and then of exegeting the text—considering, probing, and weighing the meaning of the words, phrases, paragraphs, poems, narratives, oracles, visions, and accounts that make up Scripture. Truly we must affirm that exegesis, at its best, is an act of prayerful dependence on the illuminating work of the Spirit. This does not for a moment mean that we discount the rigorous and necessary work of critical analysis, the attention due the grammar, context, and intent of the author. Yet even this work is always done in intentional dependence on the Spirit.

In other words, the critical work of biblical scholarship and study needs the corrective, or perhaps better put, the complement, that comes from the ancient practice of lectio divina, affirmed and high-lighted in the history of the church by the mystical and contemplative tradition and given currency within the contemporary church by those who insist that in our reading of Scripture, we learn what it means to not only have critical and engaged minds but also attentive, open hearts and minds that know what it means to, quite literally, read the text "in the Spirit."

This affirmation of the work of the Spirit suggests something else of utmost importance. While, without doubt, the Scriptures are a given—the same now as they were when they become the canon of the church—the reading of the text has grown and emerged. Through the gracious ministry of the Spirit, our reading of the text and our appreciation of its meaning will without doubt grow and emerge and mature and be nuanced differently precisely because the Spirit is still teaching the church and equipping the church to see new vistas in and through the ancient text. We always ask, in the language that emerges so powerfully in the book of Revelation, what is the Spirit saying to the church? (see, for example, Rev 2:7, 11). We ask this for our time and place, for this context and setting, for the here and the now, for this situation in which we live and work.

Finally, the insistence on the connection between the Spirit and the Word is a reminder to us that the prayer for illumination as preacher and congregation come to the Word in the liturgy is imperative. It is the bold affirmation that this moment, the preaching moment, is necessarily a time in the life of the church when the Christian community very intentionally leans into the Spirit. We engage the Scripture as those who are in worship, as those who come to the Scriptures from the posture and disposition of prayer. We only come to the reading of the Word and the preaching of the Word in intentional dependence on the Spirit, and we signal this in the prayer for illumination that precedes the reading and the preaching.

This means is that we never—and we need to stress this, *never*—come to the proclamation of the Word through preaching except with a prayer for illumination that precedes our reading and consideration of the Scriptures. The prayer is an essential liturgical act; a means by which we signal, but more, actually enter into a conscious awareness that we are deeply dependent on the Spirit to both read and understand and live the Scriptures we are about to engage. We might pray, "Oh Father, through your word, and through your Spirit, illumine our minds, rekindle our hearts and strengthen our wills. We pray this in the name of the risen and ascended Lord Jesus Christ." We make it clear that our reading and our preaching is in the power of the Spirit.

Furthermore, in our reading and preaching we very intentionally ask, what is the Spirit saying to the church, to this church, to this community, for such a time as this? The same congregation can come back to the same text every few years and hear it proclaimed, and each time there is an iterative quality to the experience of the text because the Spirit is at work, equipping the church to see the text, hear the text, and live the text in a way that, very possibly, the very same congregation could not have possibly seen but a few years ago. And we might change our minds on something that not too long ago we viewed as gospel truth as through the Spirit, we continue to grow, mature, and learn, and as we are ever more ready to be attentive to how the Spirit is guiding the Christian community into the truth.

Our experience of the Scriptures, of the ancient text, is not static but dynamic. Suggesting as much is not a violation of the trustworthiness or authority or consistency of the Scriptures. It is rather an affirmation that the Scriptures are always read through the lens of the risen and ascended Christ and in the Spirit, who is always leading and guiding and nudging the church to see more, to know more, and to live more fully in the gospel.

CONCLUSION

The evangelical tradition accepts quite simple and directly the words of Matthew 4:4, accepting—more, enthusiastically *believing*—that we live not by bread alone but by every word that comes from mouth of God and that the Bible was precisely this, the word that comes from God's mouth. And thus the church is sustained, fed, and encouraged by the Word.

This presumes, of course, the profound insight that emerges from the book of James: the church is not only hearing the word but doing the word (Jas 1:22). That is, the genius of the evangelical principle is not, in the end, that the Scriptures are studied and meditated upon and preached, but that the Christian and the faith community actually recognize the grace that comes through obedience. There is no other Word that can or should be used. The church lives in obedience, in deference, to the authority of Scripture, having responded in faith to the proclamation and recognized that in the preaching of the Word, the Scriptures, the church is attending to the life-giving and creative self-revelation of the triune God.

And yet while this is so very true, the most effective preaching is not that which is geared toward obedience as rather preaching that has, as its primary objective, the fostering of faith: confidence in the Word and ultimately confidence in Christ. The greatest need of the hearer on any given Sunday is not obedience but faith, for indeed the greatest obstacle to obedience is the lack of faith, and obedience is derivative of faith. Thus preaching, all preaching, regardless of the text or the occasion, is about nurturing the capacity of preacher and hearers to trust more deeply in the ascended Christ. It means trusting the Word to do what only the Word can do—slowly, gradually, and incrementally but assuredly, bring about the formation, or better put, the transformation of the people of God (see Isa 55).

The high point in evangelical worship occurs when the congregation moves to the ministry of the Word, with reverence, with hearts and minds prepared and attentive, to receive the Word with joy (1 Thess 1:6) and with meekness (Jas 1:21), ready to live in eager and joyful obedience to the Word.

THE SACRAMENTAL PRINCIPLE

BAPTISM AND THE LORD'S SUPPER are the two essential sacramental acts of the church. They are acts—gestures and symbols—ordained by Christ and, as such, a critical means by which the life and witness of the church is sustained. The church is the gathering of the baptized; the Lord's Table is the point of intense encounter between the risen Christ and the people of God. These are very *communal* acts, means by which the church nurtures its union with Christ and its communion with each other in Christian community. They are the means by which the church lives in dynamic communion with the ascended Lord Jesus Christ and knows the grace of God.

My evangelical theological tradition has developed an ambivalent if not an actual antipathy to the sacramental and to anything that appears to be a sacrament. We tend to speak of "ordinances" and do so insisting that they are not actually sacraments. For some, viewing the sacraments as a means of grace is actually a threat to the gospel. The message of my evangelical upbringing viewed faith and faith alone in response to the Word as the vehicle of salvation. This was often linked with a deep skepticism of anything physical and tangible in the Christian life, as though viewing baptism and the Lord's Supper as sacramental would undermine authentic faith. In what follows, I am going to speak of the sacramental life of the church as not only *not* a threat, but as an indispensable means by which our faith is animated and the grace of God received. And I will seek to make this point to those within my own evangelical tradition and to my pentecostal and charismatic friends.

SYMBOLS MATTER

To get a read on the matter of the sacraments, it is helpful to begin with a consideration of the meaning of symbols. In a sacramental perspective on grace and the life of the church, symbols matter a great deal. It is not uncommon for someone within my own religious tradition to speak of either baptism or the Lord's Supper as "just a symbol." This is a curious expression. My response is to say, "Of course it is symbol, but why use the word *just* as though that word keeps the symbol, the sacrament, in its place or discounts its power and significance?"

Sacraments are symbols—no more, no less. Indeed, what makes them powerful is precisely that they are symbols. More specifically, they are ordained symbols; a sacrament as a Christ-ordained symbol for the life of the church. Thus to appreciate the sacraments requires some measure of appreciation of symbol in human and in religious life.

Symbols are a vital dimension of human life; they are essential to what it means to be human and to live in society, in community with others. There are no social systems for which symbols are not both essential and, significantly, powerful. Thus it is no surprise that Christ mandated symbolic rites and gestures as a vital and essential means by which Christ would be present to the church and would sustain the life of the church. The human person is a symbol user; consequently, symbols matter to the church—and by symbols we mean both elements, such as water or wine and bread, as well as gestures, such as the act of eating or the act of participating in baptism.

In our common discourse we often use signs, photographs, and symbols to communicate with one another. Each of these—signs, photographs, and symbols—point to another reality and is a means by which we, in some form or another, actually participate in that reality. I find it helpful to consider the similarities and differences between these as part of coming to an appreciation of the character of symbol and symbolic action.

Photographs tend, as a rule, to look like that which they represent. I can speak of a photograph of my granddaughters in quite literalistic language, saying, "This is Charis and Chaia." And the one to whom I am speaking, including these two girls, have no difficulty understanding my point. No one, not even a child, suddenly thinks that my granddaughters are a piece of paper. In common parlance, we know exactly what we mean by such a phrase. And we also know this: I delight in these two granddaughters by delighting in the photograph.

A sign also points to another reality. A green light at a traffic intersection is commonly recognized as an indicator that we can proceed through the intersection. But a green light, in contrast to the photograph, does not look like that to which it points; there is nothing about proceeding that is more green than red. And yet a sign calls us to participate in something distinct from itself. I do not proceed by driving into the green light; I know that the sign and what it signifies are distinct. And yet the sign matters; it is a vital means for entering into that which is signified.

Symbols are similar in some ways to photographs and signs, but they are also different from both. In contrast to a photograph, a sign does not necessarily look like what it signifies. The wedding ring on my left hand does not look like a marriage. A nation's flag is not the map of the country. But like photographs, they do reveal another reality. They call us consider the other reality and, perhaps, to delight in or enter into that reality.

Symbols are also different from signs. Symbols are like signs in that we do not merely observe them but if we take them seriously we actually participate in that to which they point. Yes, when I see a green light, I proceed through the intersection; one might say we participate in that to which a green light points. But signs can be arbitrary; we can merely agree among ourselves that "green means go." But there is nothing inherently green about our going. In contrast, a wedding ring resonates with meaning. It "makes sense." A symbol means so much more than a (mere) sign. What makes symbols doubly significant is that they call us into a participation in that which matters to us. Symbols powerfully evoke our deepest values and associations. They are an indispensable means by which those deepest values are affirmed and formed within us.

Whether it be a national flag or a wedding ring, symbols are much more all-encompassing than photographs and signs. Like photographs and signs they communicate; but the genius of a symbol is that it calls for and fosters participation in that which is symbolized. With a sign we might *think* about something external to ourselves; with a symbol, we move beyond discourse to engagement: we *enter into* that which is symbolized. When symbols matter, we cannot respond with ambivalence; thus the reaction of Americans where their flag is burned, or the drama of the moment in a wedding when the rings are exchanged.

To participate in a symbol is to participate in that which it symbolizes. Better put, to participate in a symbol with sincerity or in Christian perspective, in faith, is to participate in that which is symbolized.

Furthermore, it is important to note also that symbols are inherently communal. A ritual is a symbolic activity that is done as a group or a community. It is something that we own *together* and do *together* that evokes deep values and aspirations, whether it be blowing out candles on a birthday cake, passing the Olympic torch, or throwing sand on a coffin. Symbols connect us with those deep values but do so in a way that connects us with each other as well. Ritual action enables us to be connected with not only the reality symbolized but also with one another as we participate in that reality together.

Without symbols, our lives would be one-dimensional. Symbols provide breadth and depth and integration. One of the deep longings of our generation is the integration of heart and mind. This is precisely what symbols do: they integrate heart and mind in our bodies. We are not mere heads or hearts; we are embodied souls.

And yet the genius of all of this is that while a sacrament is a symbol, it is not just any symbol. A sacrament is a symbol ordained by Christ. With the Word and more, in the grace of the Spirit, sacraments are symbols with power. I will address this idea more fully below in the section "Sacraments in the Life of the Church."

Before considering the theological basis for the sacraments, the following observation might be helpful. The whole point of a symbol is that it is a symbol. Thus baptism is not inherently more effective if a great deal of water is used. For the Lord's Supper, one will often hear folks insist they want a full meal, not merely a sip and a small wafer. They want something more substantial, they insist. But the point is that this is a *symbol*. And the danger is that if it looks too much like every other meal, it loses its capacity as a symbol to link heaven and earth, to draw us into another sphere of reality. That is, it no longer becomes clearly and undoubtedly a symbol. And we need to have no doubt that this is precisely a symbol. The whole point is that this is a meal in the presence of Christ and with Christ. And the value of the symbol is that, in participating, no one doubts that this is a symbol, and that thus in participating in the Lord's Supper, one is entering into a symbolic meal. It always remains a symbol—clearly so, even to children.

THE THEOLOGICAL BASIS FOR THE SACRAMENTAL PRINCIPLE: CREATION, INCARNATION, CHURCH

The theological vision or basis for the sacramental principle is anchored in three events: the creation, the incarnation, and the formation of the church. Creation, incarnation, church. Taken together they provide us with a powerful basis for recognizing that God is revealed and God's grace is known through physical, material reality, including, most notably, baptism and the Lord's Supper.

We begin with creation and recognize the significance of the created order. The great witness of the Scriptures, beginning in Genesis and then celebrated again and again in the Psalms, as a basic tenet of the Christian faith, is that "God is the maker of heaven and earth" (see for example Ps 121:2). And the Scriptures testify to the wonder that creation matters; it matters to God—indeed he declared it "good" not once but again and again and again (Gen 1). This material world, God's creation, is real; it is not an illusion. It is substantial and it is a source of delight to the Creator.

Furthermore, it is through the created order that God is known (Ps 19). God blesses and sustains humanity through the very stuff of creation, of which humanity is a part. The created order reveals God and is a means by which God is not only known but experienced. Indeed, if you love God you will love what God has made; you will revel in the very materiality or physicality of creation and see a deep continuity between your love for and participation in creation and your love for and participation in God. God and creation are distinct, of course; they are not to be confused. But as any reading of the Psalms makes clear, we know and celebrate God precisely and intentionally because God is the Creator.

A sacramental vision challenges what is essentially a pagan view of creation, a view that either discounts the material or created world, or the view that fails to appreciate that it is actually created—from God—and thus to give thanks for it (Rom 1). Even the church can so easily get in the habit of failing to appreciate the significance of God's creation. Many have grown up in religious subcultures that downplayed the creation and thus downplayed the physical. The sacramental principle is a powerful corrective. The created order is affirmed and valued and loved. It is created by God, and thus it is distinct from God. But more, God is known through the creation, a concept typically understood as *theophany*. The created order and God are distinct but inseparable.

Understandably, some have therefore concluded, given the doctrine of creation, that all of creation is sacramental and that consequently, the church and the sacraments are not needed. Some therefore suggest that all eating and drinking are acts of communion with God and with others, that all participation in the stuff of creation—every bath, every engagement with water, is purifying and grace-filled. There is potentially, they say, a sacramental element to every shared meal.

There is some truth in this observation and sensibility. And if sin had not entered into our world, we could likely take the sacramental character of the created order at face value. But the crisis of sin and evil has led the Christian theological tradition to affirm the particularity of grace. This particularity is most evident in the incarnation of the Son of God: all creation is sacramental and can only be truly sacramental when viewed and engaged through the lens of the particular act of God in Christ Jesus.

The incarnation is the ultimate expression of the revelation of God through creation, the event by which God assumed humanity in all its physicality. We come to the extraordinary realization that God is known through one human person, Jesus Christ. This is the supreme and ultimate sacramental action or event. The Word that was with God and was God took on human flesh (Jn 1:14). And through this act, God was revealed, and the grace of God was known or received on the earth. Christ became the embodiment of God on earth—flesh and blood, the very stuff of creation, now the very tangible means by which God is known. Thus, and this is a crucial point, the physicality of God's revelation in Christ is not some kind of problem or potential obstacle to knowing God. It is not that in order to know God we have to somehow bypass the oh-so-very human Jesus, to see beyond his humanity to appreciate his unique identity and the salvation that he offers. Not so; the incarnation and thus the total physicality of Jesus is the very means by which God is known.

If we want to be in communion with the Triune God, therefore, we do so by entering into communion with Jesus. Through our intimate association with Jesus—the incarnate, deeply physical Jesus—we are drawn up into fellowship with the Triune God. The physicality of Jesus, the incarnation of the Word, is the portal, you might say, by which we enter into a knowledge of God and of God's salvation.

Creation. Incarnation. We also need to speak of the church, the body of Christ.

Sacramental theology is closely tied to Christ. It is Christ whom we meet in the sacraments, and through the sacraments we are brought into fellowship and union with Christ. But the sacramental principle also brings us into the life of the church. We must begin with a realization that the church itself is not merely a religious club, not merely a gathering of Christians for religious activities; the church itself is the actual presence of Christ in the world. The church is not a human creation, but the people of God, the body of Christ and the fellowship of the Spirit, brought into being—birthed—by action of the Triune God.

Thus it can be said that they are distinct; the church is not Christ. But church and Christ are inseparable. We do not confuse the church with Christ; but then also, we know that we do not know Christ and live in fellowship with Christ—from a sacramental perspective—unless we are in fellowship with the church. This means that we can speak of the sacramental character of the church itself. We participate in the life of Christ through engagement with the church. The church is a continuing sign and symbol of the Risen Christ; the community of faith is the body of Christ, a living and tangible witness on the earth to the ascended Lord.

It is very important to stress that the sacraments are the work of God. They are not so much human actions as divine workings in and through the church. But that is precisely the point; they are in and through the church. Even though in the end they do not belong to the church, they are *within* the church. While they are in a sense the actions of the church, they are church actions only as a response to the primary actor, who necessarily is God.

It therefore follows that since these actions are located within the church, these are not private or family acts or rituals; they belong within the church and thus the authority for their administration lies with the church. They are only administered by the church—that is, by those so authorized by the church; they are not a private matter for individuals to take into their own hands.

Creation. Incarnation. Church. The church takes water, wine, and bread—the very stuff of life, through actions ordained by Christ—sanctifies them (by the Word and by the Spirit), so that they might be drawn into fellowship with Christ and with his church and thus be drawn into fellowship with the Triune God.

And the focal point is Christ. The sacraments are the very means by which we are brought into union with Christ. Thus to despise the sacraments is to despise Christ, for they re-present Christ and have been instituted by Christ to communicate his saving grace. In these acts we are united with *Christ* in his death and resurrection; we are in communion with *Christ* (Rom 6; 1 Cor 10). The central dynamic of the liturgical life of the church and of its sacramental life is this: we live in dynamic, intimate, and immediate fellowship with the living, ascended Christ. The ideal then is that the church would grow to appreciate that the sacraments are really nothing other than a God-ordained means by which the church lives in communion with the living Christ. This means that we believe, know, feel, and live in the ever present dynamic that Christ is present to the church as the ascended Lord, in real time. More specifically, Christ is present to the church through the sacraments.

This sequence of creation, incarnation, and church presumes something fundamental about the nature of the human person: we are embodied souls; we are animated bodies. There is a deep physicality to our Christian identity and thus to Christian spirituality. There is a profound sense that there is no redemption until we know the redemption of our bodies. Our bodies are not secondary or incidental to our knowledge of the salvation of God. Indeed, if our faith in Christ is not embodied and if our experience of the grace of God does not happen in our bodies, we can legitimately ask whether it "took" at all. We do not need to fear focused discussion on our embodiment. The New Testament writers do not seem to fear this physicality out of a concern that it will undermine the internal character of Christian spirituality. They speak as though it is by baptism that we are incorporated into the community of faith. Even though Paul insists that it is only by faith that we are justified, he nevertheless insists that we put on Christ by baptism (Gal 3:26-28). We see this same perspective reinforced in Romans 6, with the apostle Paul's telling observation that we are united with Christ, in his death and resurrection, very precisely through baptism. We are flesh and blood creatures. We can only worship in the body and only respond to God in the body. Actually, unless our worship is embodied it is not true worship. We do not worship as angels worship; we are higher than angels and worship, therefore, in our full embodiment, with our senses fully engaged.

The great danger in worship—especially the worship of the modern era—is that worship become entirely an intellectual affair or nothing more than sentimental experience. Worship becomes unreal or disengaged, intellectual or sentimental, but not truly able to foster genuine koinonia, or fellowship, with God. All too easily it is overly verbal, largely the communication of information, because it only takes account of the auditory and does not include sight, taste, smell, and movement. Or it is overly sentimental, catering to mere affect or emotion, little more than entertainment that seeks positive or good feelings. The sacraments ground us, fostering integration rather than bifurcation of head and heart.

It is so easy for worship to be purely didactic, information communicated verbally or visually, or sentimental, mere manipulation of the worshiper's heart strings. And it is also so very easy for worship to become mere observation of that which is happening on the "stage" as those present are moved by a charismatic speaker or entertained by a powerful and skilled worship band. The corrective is found through the sacraments, which integrate and ground our worship. With the sacraments we move from being observers to participants; we learn what it means to know the integration of heart and mind and the transforming grace of God that comes to us through the sacramental actions of the church.

Evangelical church leaders and pastors are typically very keen to affirm the need for discipleship, spiritual growth, and transformation. All good, of course! But the irony for me is that evangelical worship is typically so geared to either the didactic or the sentimental that transformation does not occur. And the missing ingredient, often—not always, but often—is the church's observance of sacraments. What needs to be urgently reaffirmed is that the sacraments are not incidental to the spiritual life. The sacraments are not mere tokens. They are the very means by which the church lives; the life of the church depends on them. They are crucial to our commitment to spiritual formation and discipleship.

I have attended whole conferences on spiritual formation and discipleship that proceeded without a single reference to the sacraments. For those of a sacramental tradition this makes no sense: we make disciples through baptism and teaching (Mt 28), and the essential spiritual food for spiritual growth is found in the very body of Christ that is received at the Table. We are formed by Word and Table. As a university president, I am deeply aware of how crucial it is that undergraduate students embrace these years as a season of intentional and focused spiritual growth and formation. It only follows that this would be a season of life when being present to the Lord's Table is doubly important.

THE SACRAMENTAL LIFE OF THE CHURCH

In sacramental actions, we take the stuff of creation and, in the power of Word and Spirit, know the revelation and grace of God in and through that which God has made. And as already noted, the assumption is fairly straightforward: a sacrament is a Christ-ordained *gesture*—not just the water, but actual immersion or sprinkling with that water; not just bread and wine, but bread and wine consumed.

We need to consider the two central and defining sacramental acts of the church, baptism and the Lord's Supper. But first it is important to acknowledge that many traditions either speak of other sacraments or have other rites or symbolic gestures that have a sacramental quality to them.

Catholic Christians, for example, have lived with a long tradition following Peter Lombard, who, between 1155 and 1158, argued in his "Sentences" for seven sacraments: baptism, confirmation, Eucharist, penance, marriage, ordination, and extreme unction. This was formally endorsed in the Council of Florence in 1439. Some Anabaptist groups have practiced and continue to practice foot washing as a sacrament because they feel it can be argued that this too was ordained by Christ. And many holiness and pentecostal traditions include the practice of anointing the sick.

Indeed, many church communions have rites or rituals that have a distinctly sacramental character to them, the laying on of hands in ordination; the basin of water and the hands of one who humbly kneels to wash the feet of another; the rite of marriage and the exchange of rings. In each case there is a physical, tangible act by which the church leans into the grace of God.

But on the whole, the Protestant and evangelical tradition has affirmed with Calvin that baptism is the rite "of initiation into the faith, and the Lord's Supper the constant aliment by which Christ spiritually feeds his family of believers. . . . Besides these two, no other has been instituted by God, and no other ought to be recognized by the assembly of the faithful." The rite of initiation, the rite of nurture.

Earlier in his ministry, Martin Luther insisted contra the Council of Florence that there were only three sacraments, baptism, Eucharist, and penance. But he later revised his opinion for precisely the reason noted above: a sacrament is a rite that is clearly ordained by Christ, affirming that "there are only two sacraments in the church of God—baptism and bread. For only in these two do we find the divinely instituted sign and the promise of the forgiveness of sins."

And even within the Catholic tradition, there is a recognition that these two are the "dominical" sacraments, meaning that they are clearly ordained by Christ. Thus, while there may be other actions of the church that have a sacramental character to them, the two—baptism as a rite of initiation and the Lord' Supper as the rite by which the church is sustained in union with Christ—anchor the faith of the church. They lie at the heart of the sacramental principle as the non-negotiable practices by which the church is the church. As Lesslie Newbigin puts it, "It belongs to the heart of the biblical doctrine of the church that our incorporation in Christ is by faith, so it is no less central to this doctrine that our incorporation is by baptism into a visible fellowship . . . and that our participation in the life of the body is maintained by our sharing in the one loaf and the one cup in one undivided fellowship." We are in Christ, individually and corporately, through baptism and Holy Communion.

Baptism, rite of initiation. Baptism is the rite of Christian initiation. The witness of the New Testament suggests that for the early church there was no such thing as an unbaptized Christian. And similarly, the Scriptures do not seem to have any problem linking baptism directly with the experience of God's forgiveness, whether it is the call of Acts 2:38 or Paul's testimony to his own conversion when he speaks of how, when he stumbled into Damascus blind and struck by the encounter with Christ, Ananias says to him, "Get up, be baptized, and have your sins washed away, calling on his name" (Acts 22:16).

And Peter can simply and forthrightly speak of baptism as that which "now saves you" (1 Pet 3:21). From a sacramental perspective, to speak in such a manner is not a problem, for to participate in the symbol is to participate in that which is symbolized. Just as Jesus can speak of the bread, "this is my body," so we can speak of the waters of baptism as that by which we know the forgiveness of sins and are brought into fellowship with Christ and with his church. We are incorporated into a new order of life. Our identity, our "family," our way of being, all change. Very certainly we signal this when we accept the act of baptism, when we submit to the baptismal waters. But more, what occurs is that God acts through these waters to bring us into fellowship with himself and his people.

Is there a one-to-one link or correlation between baptism and the salvation of God? Well, yes and no. On the one hand, a case can be made that until we are baptized, the grace of God is not embodied within us. And if it is not embodied, it does not truly become us. And yet, we can affirm the priority of the interior and baptism might not be linked immediately to the experience of grace, but rather be a signal of what God is doing in our lives, the God who is active and present to us before and after our baptism. In other words, we can fully affirm the sacramental character of the grace of God but not assume that there is a causal link or, at least, affirm that the link is subtler. Our actual experience of the regenerating grace of God may not be occasioned, causally or directly, by our baptism. This does not for a moment discount the importance or power of baptism; it merely highlights that God's work in our lives may not be linked immediately and directly to our work or the work of the church in baptism.

The Lord's Supper, the church in fellowship with the ascended Lord. From baptism, we come to the meal. For the sacramental perspective, the Lord's Table is the focal point of Christian worship. Here, in this meal, Christ—the risen and ascended Lord—meets his disciples in real time. We can speak of this meal as a memorial, as an act of communion with Christ and his church, as the table of mercy and forgiveness, as the venue where we renew our baptismal identity and are nourished for the road, and as an act by which the church anticipates the consummation of the reign of Christ. And, of course, the whole event is infused with thanksgiving; it is a holy Eucharist.

Here too, as in baptism, there is no avoiding the profound physicality of this act of eating and drinking. Nothing is gained by downplaying this. We remember that the genius of the sacramental vision is that the glory and grace of God is revealed to us and comes to us through materiality and that the incarnation, the embodied Word of God, the real live *physical* Jesus, is the means by which God's grace is known.

The Lord's Supper is not an act of mere mental assent, as though the bread is only a token, a kind of mnemonic device to help the Christian remember Jesus. To the contrary, in the language of the apostle Paul, the Lord's Supper is a meal in which we are in communion—koinonia, fellowship—with Jesus' body. When we take the cup, we enter into fellowship with his blood (1 Cor 10:14-17). Non-sacramentalists or those who are ambivalent about the sacramental perspective tend to resist this one-to-one link between our eating and drinking and the body and blood of Jesus. But the witness of the New Testament is unavoidable in this regard. And more, this resistance is as much as anything a failure to appreciate the deep physicality of our faith.

The early church, we read, devoted themselves to "the breaking of bread," Luke's way of speaking of the Lord's Supper (Acts 2:42). And the weight of the evidence suggests that they celebrated the Table each time they gathered (Acts 20:7). The evidence is for many not conclusive, and thus they see no reason to celebrate the Lord's Supper weekly. But there is no doubt that the post-Apostolic church celebrated the Lord's Supper weekly. And there is also no doubt that worship is grounded, embodied, when the full sacramental life of the church is embraced. In other words, baptism is indispensable to the initiation into faith; the Lord's Table is essential for the life of faith and thus for the worship of the church.

Taken together, baptism and the Lord's Supper are the ordained means by which we are drawn into life with Christ. In baptism we are united with Christ in his death and resurrection (Rom 6:4); in the Lord's Supper, we meet Christ and are in fellowship with Christ. In other words, these are not ends in themselves. Their meaning and their power are intimately and directly linked with the glory and presence of the ascended Christ. Thus, in the Lord's Supper, we meet Jesus. Our ultimate longing and encounter is not with bread and cup, but with the risen Lord.

SACRAMENTS AND THE WORD, SACRAMENTS AND THE SPIRIT

A vital and essential consideration is that the sacraments do not stand or function in isolation from the Word or the Spirit. Whenever we speak of either baptism or the Lord's Supper, we must also speak of Word, and we must speak of the Holy Spirit. And this might, of course, serve as a gentle corrective for those of a more sacramental persuasion who may not have a fulsome appreciation of the place of Word and Spirit in the life of the church.

First, the sacraments always function in tandem with the Word. Always. They have no power—significance—on their own, but only in complement to the Word. On the one hand, the sacraments are a visual demonstration of the gospel, a non-verbal means by which the gospel is proclaimed. Baptism, as a symbol, is a powerful witness to the cleansing power of the gospel. The Lord's Supper speaks of both the radical hospitality of Christ Jesus and the nourishment which Christ provides for his disciples. But more, the Word precedes, informs, and sanctifies the sacramental action. So baptism necessarily *follows* the proclamation of the gospel heard and received in faith. It is an intentional act of response to the Word. The Word preached gives meaning and content and power to the immersion in the waters of baptism. The sequence is important: baptism follows the proclamation of the Word.

Some will no doubt wonder if this has implications for whether or not it is appropriate to practice the baptism of infants. Typically, and it is no coincidence, more sacramental traditions practice infant baptism. And just as typically, Evangelicals have historically protested and insisted that baptism only has significance when it is informed and preceded by the Word—when the candidate for baptism is able to respond personally and intentionally to the Word. This is not the place to resolve this dispute; but we can insist on the following: infant baptism necessarily assumes that "Word" that will come—through the catechism of the young person who moves towards an adult affirmation of their faith. This encounter with the Word, studied, preached, known, and obeyed is essential to the efficacy of their baptism.

In like fashion, the church has always recognized that there are two great movements in Christian worship—the Word read, proclaimed, and then the Table, following the Word. Word and Table. Church groups that rather arbitrarily put the Lord's Supper earlier in the service, before the reading of Scripture or the sermon, inadvertently signal that somehow the Table, the Holy Meal, stands on its own. But in the very same way that baptism necessarily follows evangelism, even so the Lord's Supper necessarily follows the proclamation of the Word.

The words of institution are essential to the celebration of the Lord's Supper. But in the end, what makes this meal the meal of the Lord, who meets his people in real time, is the Word; it is the Word that sanctifies the waters of baptism and the Word that sanctifies the bread and wine. Thus in the book of Ephesians, the apostle speaks of the church cleansed by the "washing of water by the word" (Eph 5:26). The power of the water, one would rightly conclude, is linked directly to the effectiveness of the Word. The church is called to make disciples by baptism *and* teaching (Mt 28:19-20); the two necessarily go together.

But here, those of a sacramental tradition need to lean into the wisdom of the evangelical theological and spiritual tradition. Preaching, as the complement to the sacraments, only has significance if it actually commends and exposits the text of Scripture. Those of more sacramental traditions have no lack of Scripture readings; indeed, they typically have four readings—the Old Testament, a Psalm, the Epistles and then the climatic reading of the Gospels. This is excellent. But then frequently the sermon seems to have only a vague connection to those readings. As often as not, it would seem that the Scripture readings for the day are an occasion for the preacher to expound on a key or vital theme, perhaps a pet theme, even. What is preached is not the Scriptures—an idea or a principle, but not the Scriptures themselves.

The power of the sacraments is that they are informed by the Scriptures read and preached; the power of preaching is that the text is preached and that the preacher clearly has no other agenda but to draw people into the Scriptures, to know the Word, to feel the full force of the Word, and to know the grace of living under the Word. Then from that disposition, worshipers move to the celebration of the Eucharist.

And as a side note, let me suggest the following. Each celebration of the rites of baptism and the Lord's Supper needs to include words of welcome and explanation, along with words of institution. In this regard, we can be clear and concise, but we do not need to be overly verbal. We certainly do not need a second sermon, and we do not need an extended explanation of the meaning of these symbols. We have already heard a sermon; we do not need more and more words. The power of the sacrament, as with any symbol, lies not in our explanations but in the symbol itself. Sometimes, in some circles, the power of symbol or sacrament is diminished by too much explaining.

Second, the Spirit and the sacraments are also inseparable. While the sacraments are located in the church, as already noted, they are not ultimately the actions of the church. They are, of course, the actions of the faith community; we baptize one another and we take bread and cup and we participate in the ritual actions. But ultimately and essentially we affirm that the sacraments are the acts of God, who in the power of the Spirit draws us into union with Christ. Yes, we are baptized by the hands of the ordained minister; yes, we eat and drink the elements handed to us by our sisters and brothers. But if there is grace—if the symbolic rites have any meaning—it is because of the gracious work of the Spirit.

The great danger in the sacramental acts is that we might begin to think of them or even assume that they are our acts. While they are, it is only in a secondary sense that they are the acts of the Christian and of the church. They are first and ultimately the acts of God, who graces his church in Christ by—and this is the crucial piece—the power of the Spirit. We see a link between water and Spirit in John 3, but also Titus 3:5, which speaks of "the water of rebirth and renewal by the Holy Spirit." The two necessarily are twinned.

This must be referenced; we need to speak to this even in the liturgy itself. When it comes to the sacraments, two things are imperative: the sacrament follows the Word, for the Word informs and sanctifies the sacrament. We affirm Word and sacrament in tandem. But then we also affirm Spirit and sacrament—again, in tandem. And so we come to the sacrament with the prayer "come, Holy Spirit come." Come, Holy Spirit, and take these physical and tangible things—bread, cup, water—so that they might be a means of grace to the people of God. The church must call for and affirm the presence of the Spirit in the sacramental actions of the church. There is an ancient word for this prayer, *epiclēsis*. And it is essential. In many respects, it makes all the difference. It is a reminder that when we come to the Lord's Table, we come in response to the prompting of the Spirit, we come in the Spirit and in coming we are graced by the Spirit. The sacraments are a means by which we walk in the Spirit; all that we long for of the Spirit is given to us in this meal. And further, the Spirit is the one who makes the sacraments sacramental.

We need to make it abundantly clear that we come to both Word—the meditation on the Word and the public proclamation of the Word—and sacrament "in the Spirit." When we come to the Table, as Rowan Williams puts it so well, the same Spirit who brought Jesus into the world, conceived in the womb of Mary, and who brings new birth to those called of God, "'overshadows' the bread and wine and fills them with new life." Thus Williams writes, speaking of the Eucharist, "we pray in the Holy Spirit and we receive gifts that the Holy Spirit has made to be vehicles of this life." Therefore Williams stresses, echoing the perspective of the Eastern Church, the high moment in the celebration of the Lord's Supper is not the recounting of what happened at the Last Supper—which, of course, is so very important and essential—but rather, the climatic prayer when we ask the Holy Spirit to come upon the elements that they might indeed be the gifts of God for the people of God.

Evangelicals can so easily default to a fundamentalism that absolutizes the words of Scripture—the scourge of biblicism. Sacramentalists tend to absolutize the rites and rituals of the church, so that the symbols—such as bread and cup—become the reality rather than a means by which we know the reality. With a dynamic theology of the Spirit, we can affirm that the Spirit, informing Word and sacrament, makes them a means of grace. As Simon Chan puts it, "Without active participation and the Spirit's presence, the liturgy of the Word becomes mere intellectualism; the liturgy of the sacrament becomes mere ritualism."

Thus I must register a subtle protest, not only against those traditions that have no reference to the Holy Spirit's presence, work, and power, either in baptism or the Lord's Supper, but also those congregations within perhaps Anglican or Episcopalian circles that choose the liturgy of the Iona Community in Scotland, on the thought that this liturgy is more accessible to non-Anglicans. And my protest is simple and straightforward regarding the Iona liturgy: Where is the *epiclēsis*? When I attend a worship service and in the celebration of the Lord's Table there is no reference to the Spirit, I am struck by the stunning gap. It simply makes no sense to me. And I could say the same about baptism which, in the end, means nothing apart of the work of the Spirit in the life of the one being initiated into Christian faith and community. We need to make this explicit. Without the *epiclēsis*—the prayer "come, Holy Spirit come"—we in effect signal that these actions are human work and no more.

In the end, in humble dependence on the Spirit, we enter into the waters of baptism and come to the Table, eager to trust more, eager to grow in faith (Jas 1:21). As with the Word, humility is always the crucial disposition for those who come to the Lord's Table. We come trusting; we come with whatever measure of faith we have. And we ask that through the acts of baptism and the Lord's Table, we would grow in deeper dependence upon the grace of God.

On the one hand, the sacraments are the expression of our faith. We come to the Table believing in Christ and trusting that Christ receives us and grants us his grace. And yet it is also important to stress that the sacraments strengthen our faith; we come in response to the Word, in dependence on the Spirit, and eager for our faith to be not merely internal but actually embodied.

And yes, there are times when we find that our faith is weak as we struggle to believe and trust. Yet we still come to the Table, and the important point is that the efficacy of the Table is not dependent on the quality of our faith. Thanks be to God! We can come even when our faith is feeble. But we come, and we come in obedience. And what we find is that in coming, our faith is strengthened. We come, leaning into the Word and the Spirit, recognizing that we are coming along with the company of God's people. What carries the day is not the quality or level of our faith, but the Word and the Spirit and the company of people who are the body of Christ.

SACRAMENTAL SPIRITUALITY

Finally, two more points conclude these observations on the sacramental perspective on the Christian faith.

First, a vital sacramental perspective consistently fosters a more intentional and dynamic theology of the church. This obviously reflects the appreciation of the sacramental character of the church itself. As noted, a sacramental perspective assumes that the church itself has a sacramental character to it and that, of course, there is only one church. The creedal affirmation that the church is "one, holy, catholic, and apostolic" has profound implications for ecumenism. Sacramental Christians are thus—or perhaps better, tend to be— more ecumenically oriented; they recognize that for all its flaws, the church is still the body of Christ. Church division or separation tears at the very fabric that is the body of Christ, and any kind of schism, even if necessary, is tragic and to be avoided at all costs. Typically, also, those of a sacramental perspective will lean into the apostolicity of the church—recognizing the importance of fellowship with those communions that are in historic fellowship with the apostles. And in this regard, these more sacramental traditions take ordination seriously, recognizing its sacramental perspective—the ordained one stands in the place of Christ at the table, a kind of surrogate Christ, or better put, an icon of Christ.

And speaking of the church, those of a more sacramental persuasion not only see themselves to be in sacramental communion with the whole historic church, back to the apostles, but also in dynamic fellowship with those who have already crossed over—the saints, the "cloud of witnesses" that surrounds the contemporary Christian community (Heb 12:1). And the assumption is that we are in real-time fellowship with these saints, meaning that they are still dynamically present to the church, praying with the church, and being a continued source of inspiration to the church, most notably through the lives of the saints.

And second, one will also find that those of a sacramental perspective tend to be more comfortable with the physical expressions of faith, such as pilgrimages, the sign of the cross, the use of incense to indicate the prayers of the people of God. They are more comfortable speaking of sacred spaces and holy water. They find that God reveals God's very self and God's grace not merely in baptism and the Lord's Table but in other physical and tangible manifestations of God's holy presence. A pilgrimage becomes a means of grace as through the act of walking, one embodies the inner journey of faith. The sign of the cross becomes an essential means by which one identifies with the cross of Christ. And holy water is a subtle but potentially powerful means of living again in the grace of one's baptism. Are these essential? Not at all. But for those of a sacramental persuasion, they are important means and signs by which we live an embodied faith in Christ.

CONCLUSION

When all is said and done, any reflection on the sacraments brings us back to two extraordinary gifts—gifts from God, for the people of God—two gifts that make the church the church: baptism and the Lord's Supper. It behooves us to receive both in faith and thanksgiving. And it is imperative that we appreciate that through these symbols, Christ is present to his people, and that this is a transformative presence. In worship, the symbol and the reality are one. Baptism then becomes the focal point of one's initiation into the faith. And the Lord's Supper, the Eucharist, becomes the focal point, the high point, of the gathering of the people of God for worship.

SIX

THE PENTECOST PRINCIPLE

Between Galatians 5:16 and Galatians 6:10 we have a string of references to the dynamic of the Spirit's immediate presence and impact both in the lives of Christian believers and the life of the church. The segment opens with a call to "live by the Spirit" (Gal 5:16) that seems to be linked with being "led by the Spirit" (Gal 5:18). Then we have the clear expectation that Christian believers and indeed the Christian community will bear the fruit of the Spirit: "love, joy, peace, patience, kindness, generosity, faithfulness, gentleness, and self-control" (Gal 5:22-23).

Then the apostle comes back to the opening baseline and speaks of living by the Spirit, which is here linked with being "guided by the Spirit" (Gal 5:25). And all of this is seemingly made possible because, as he puts it in Galatians 6:1, we have "received the Spirit" and so we can correct others, as necessary, with gentleness. And finally there is the observation that those who do well and live in generous community are those who "sow to the Spirit" (Gal 6:8).

When taken together, this series of observations and exhortations is a clear call to intentionality, urging readers to a greater level of astuteness regarding our experience of the Holy Spirit. The assumption of this diversity of calls to live in the Spirit assumes that this is the only way to live as a Christian and that this is what it means to live in community. We are only truly the church when we live, together, in the fellowship of the Spirit. And if we manage to live in community, it will be because we learn to live in the Spirit, walk in the Spirit, be led by the Spirit, and bear the fruit of the Spirit.

Most notably, implied in these invitations and exhortations from the book of Galatians are an immediacy and an intimacy between the church and the Holy Spirit. This is exemplified in the book of Acts. And it speaks of what might be termed "the Pentecost principle" that the Christian life is lived in the grace and power of the Holy Spirit and that this is experienced immediately. It is a sensible knowledge, a felt knowledge and awareness of the Third person of the Holy Trinity.

Both evangelical and sacramentally oriented Christians would affirm the triunity of God and the indispensability of the Spirit for the life and witness of the church and the individual Christian. But the challenge from those of pentecostal persuasion to the evangelical and the more sacramental Christian is that the witness of the Scriptures and the history of the church suggests that we are invited—better put, *called*—to live in conscious awareness of the Spirit in our lives and in radical dependence on the Spirit to live our lives. Pentecostal Christians observe that so many self-identified Christians tend to live out their lives on a mundane level—meaning not ordinary or routine but rather with an earthly orientation that gives little or any evidence of a life lived in actual communion with the Living God, a communion that is made possible through the gift of the Spirit. Let me stress this point: the problem is not that lives are ordinary; to the contrary we must speak of the presence of the Spirit very specifically in the ordinary. The problem or issue at hand is that it would seem that for so many Christians, they live without an awareness, on any level, of the immediacy of God in their lives.

They live, one might say, in a binitarian rather than a trinitarian world; they have, at best, a truncated pneumatology. They have little consciousness of the Spirit's agency in their lives.

The Pentecost principle would suggest that this is not as it should be. Rather, the Spirit is a person and a full member of the Trinity, and, further, the Spirit is the gift from the Father, through the Son, the one by whom we live in union with Christ, dwell in his love, and are empowered to live in community and to fulfill our respective vocations. The church is the church in the power of the Spirit as it fulfills both its call to unity and the call to mission. But more, that the Spirit is present—immediately and thus graciously—touching the very heart and core of our human identity.

THE HISTORIC WITNESS TO THE IMMEDIACY OF THE SPIRIT

The gift of the various charismatic renewal movements of the last century has been to affirm the immediacy of the Spirit in the life of the Christian and in the life of the church. But it is important to stress that this is not a new awareness or recent discovery. Throughout the history of the church there has been a solid and clear witness—a dynamic thread, or better, a stream if not a full river—that has affirmed both the possibility of this immediacy and its essentialness to the church and for each Christian. From the church fathers to the Medieval mystics to the 16th century Catholic Reformers, including John of the Cross, Teresa of Avila, and Ignatius Loyola, and then on to John and Charles Wesley, and, with many other voices along the way, to the contemporary charismatic communities and movements that make up a huge segment of the global Christian community in this century, these voices and movements typically recognized the importance not only of experience but also, particularly, experience that could be described as "movements of the heart." As such they affirmed the vital place of affect and emotion in the life of the church and the life of the individual Christian. They speak collectively of the Pentecost principle—that the Spirit witnesses with our spirits (Rom 8:16), that the Spirit pours the love of God into our hearts (Rom 5:5), and that the genius of the spiritual life is to know the grace of walking in and living by the Spirit.

Consider, for example, Origen of Alexandria (AD 185–254), who was in many respects the most influential theologian in the church prior to Augustine. He is known to us through the ecclesiastical history written by Eusebius, who helps us appreciate that Origen's immediate context was the persecuted church, including his own experience of tribulation. Origen's most significant contribution on the theme of the immediacy of the Spirit and of God is found in his reflections on prayer and discernment in two works, *Spirit and Fire* and *On Prayer*. In both he stresses that prayer is not merely petition, but actual participation in the life of God. And the crucial thing in this regard is that we learn to be open to and responsive to the Spirit. Sin is powerful, Origin stresses, but with discipline and practice, we can learn what it means to be open to the Spirit and in turn, we can learn to discern the presence of the Spirit in our lives.

Origen speaks of the "discernment of spirits," providing perhaps the earliest source we have that uses this language or phrase. He speaks of two "spirits" and suggests that each person has something like a good angel and a personal devil, a kind of particular expression of the Spirit of God who calls us to the good, and the "satanic spirit" that would destroy us. His particular emphasis is that the fruit of the "good spirit" is peace and the actions that arise from peace. And thus peace—he actually uses the language of "consolation"—is the true home, the resting place of the soul. In peace we have, as he puts it, "a vision into the true nature of things." In peace we see rightly—peace not as the way of ease but rather a peace in the very midst of pain and suffering, wherein we are sustained by an awareness of the love of God, a love that we know through the inner working of the Spirit in our hearts.

Thus the crucial question for Origen is the disposition of the heart. We need to learn, through discipline and practice, receptivity and discernment; we learn the way of the Spirit over time through the challenges and turmoils of life.

Bernard of Clairvaux (AD 1090–1153) was the most influential churchman of his generation, was both theologian and mystic, and left a lasting impact in the renewal of monastic orders. And what catches our attention early on in reading Bernard is his stress on the immediacy of our experience of God, which is experienced as the love of God. He emphasizes both heart and mind, stressing the vital place of the heart and of the affections in Christian experience, captured in the line for which he is justly famous: "Instruction makes us learned, but feeling makes us wise." For Bernard, theology is not about intellect in the end but rather an experiential knowledge of God. We are designed to know the experiential love of God—the experience of the love of God not merely knowledge about the love of God—and to respond in kind to this love. This is our true home.

And to this end, he speaks of fervor—of knowing God passionately in our hearts—as an ordered passion. Spiritual fervor without discernment is dangerous; we cannot be naive to the presence of evil in the world and in our hearts. Though he does not reference the closing verses of 1 Thessalonians 5, he speaks in like matter of the need for an eager and open heart—a passionate heart that does not limit or quench the Spirit—but then also of the need for discernment. We cannot be naïve and trust every movement of the heart. Deep and radical openness to the Spirit leads not to uncritical judgements but to growth in wisdom and understanding.

When we come to the sixteenth century, a powerful triad of spiritual writers arises from Spain—forces for renewal in the Catholic Reformation, counterparts to the major leaders of the northern and Protestant Reformation. I think here of John of the Cross (AD 1542–1591), Teresa of Avila (AD 1515–1582), and Ignatius Loyola (AD 1491–1556). Ignatius is best known as the founder of the Society of Jesus (Jesuit) but also as the author of the classic guide to directed prayer, the *Spiritual Exercises*. While founding an extraordinary missionary order, Ignatius also articulated a distinctive spiritual vision: the contemplative vision of Christ was the essential complement to apostolic witness.

Ignatian spirituality is a spirituality of response to the initiative of the Holy Spirit. The genius of the *Exercises* is that we learn to be attentive the work of the Spirit whose presence is known in the movement of our hearts. Most notably, the pray-er learns to be attentive to the presence and meaning of consolation and desolation.

But, and this is crucial, this response to the Spirit arises from a personal and immediate encounter with Christ. This is done not through thinking about Jesus—the idea of Jesus or even the powerful idea that Christ is died and risen—but by an actual encounter with the ascended, risen Christ who is revealed to us through the Gospel narratives' depiction of the life, death, and resurrection of Jesus. And thus those who pray seek to know Christ and have their minds saturated by the Spirit of Christ, the same Spirit who enables Jesus to do the will of the Father. This, then, is not a spirituality of meditation on Christ and the life of Christ as a kind of supreme ethical model, a kind of "what would Jesus do?" approach that assumes guidance in the Christian life is simply a matter of determining what Jesus would do in a given situation. Rather for the Ignatian and mystical tradition, our engagement with the world arises out of an immediate and intimate experience of Christ. We know the mind of Christ because we have met Christ and been with Christ. A parallel in the experience of a Christian community is that a worship service is not an encounter with an idea but with a person, the Lord Jesus Christ, in real time.

And the evidence that we have met Christ—in real time? That we dwell in the love of Christ and that we move into the world with a resilient and abiding joy.

I choose Ignatius Loyola as a representative of the mystical theological and spiritual tradition because of the radical christocentricity of Ignatian spirituality and its deep commitment to mission and engagement with the world. And the two go together; the encounter with Christ, the contemplative vision, made possible through the gracious ministry of the Spirit, should and will consistently foster dynamic engagement with the world.

But the main point I am making here is that there is a consistent stream or thread in the history of the church that has stressed both the potential of immediacy with God—indeed not only the potential but the priority.

These kinds of sensibilities have always unsettled the mainstream of the church. The fifteenth and sixteenth century *alumbrados* were suppressed by the Catholic Inquisition largely for their teaching that immediate access to God was possible, suggesting that the church could be bypassed. Indeed, Ignatius Loyola received an admonition when there was a charge laid against him for teaching what some thought came precariously close to this sect.

Both John Calvin and Martin Luther were also deeply skeptical of any teaching that suggested the possibility of an immediate experience of God. Luther had an ongoing battle with the "spiritualists" from the town of Zwickau, preachers who were inspired by the teachings of Thomas Müntzer, one of the Anabaptist teachers who insisted that

Christians could live by a daily interior experience of God's Word. Luther, of course, insisted that any movement that neglected or discounted the objective witness of Scripture or life in community was immediately suspect. Calvin, in like manner, had to fend off radical sectors of the Swiss Reformation that sought inner illumination apart from the Scriptures. These various fringe elements without doubt needed correction; they were a problem. But, perhaps unfortunately, Luther and Calvin could not incorporate into their own teaching a legitimate expression of the inner illuminating grace of God. It was not to be, and the heirs of the Protestant Reformation—notably those of a more evangelical persuasion with a defining emphasis on the priority of the Word—have consistently been rather suspicious of anything that was not mediated through the Scriptures.

And yet as noted, there has always been a witness in the history of the church to the immediacy of the experience of the Spirit—mystics, enthusiasts, Wesleyans, pietists—and, of course, in the last two centuries, we have the nineteenth century holiness movement and the Pentecostal and charismatic revolution in the twentieth century.

Pentecostalism is the fastest growing religious movement in history, now pervasively present in Latin America and Africa. And it has had a profound influence within major Christian denominations, such that we can speak, for example, of a whole charismatic stream within Roman Catholicism. The movement is marked by ecstatic worship, tongues-speaking, miraculous healings, and enthusiastic missionary witness. Notable also is that, in many contexts, the movement lacks of formalized governance structures with its appeal to spontaneity.

It is relatively easy to critique the pentecostal movement. We can speak of the vulnerability to new revelations or to the neglect of the creedal heritage of the church. We can speak of faith communities that are overly focused on charismatic personalities with little real accountability for their ministries. We can speak of anti-intellectualism or a propensity for divisiveness. All of these might be legitimate concerns about either historic mysticism or the contemporary Pentecostal. The danger, though, is being dismissive and thus missing out on something that is fundamental to the life of the church and the individual Christian.

At its best, the charismatic and pentecostal movement has emphasized that the spiritual world is *immediate*—very much real and very much at hand—and that the Holy Spirit has and is infusing the creation, the church, and potentially each individual Christian believer with divine grace. Concerns arise, of course, when the sacraments and biblical preaching are neglected, when religious leaders lack accountability, or when a prosperity gospel co-opts the gospel of the cross. But this should not discourage the church from seeking and living in dynamic fellowship with the Spirit, a fellowship that will be evident in two things, love—the experience of God's love that radiates within the faith community and to the world—and second, the experience of a deep and resilient joy.

THE THEOLOGICAL FOUNDATIONS
FOR THE PENTECOST PRINCIPLE

The pentecostal principle is built on a foundation that is both theological and experiential, and it finds expression not only in the life of the church but also in an appreciation of the ways of the Spirit within the created order as a whole.

Two sendings. First, the theological foundation for the pentecostal principle arises from the observation, going all the way back to the early church, that the Scriptures witness to two sendings, the sending of the Son and the sending of the Spirit. Robert Louis Wilken in his study of early Christian worship and spirituality notes that these two defining events informed the worship and the prayers of the early church such that there was a deep awareness of the incarnation and then Pentecost as distinct but complementary events. Reference was often made to Galatians 4:4-7:

> But when the fullness of time had come, God sent his Son, born of a woman, born under the law, in order to redeem those who were under the law, so that we might receive adoption as children. And because you are children, God has sent the Spirit of his Son into our hearts, crying "Abba! Father!" So you are no longer a slave but a child, and if a child then also an heir, through God.

In time the early church came to view the Feast of Pentecost as an integral part of the church calendar, celebrating the gift of the Spirit with the same attention that they would have given to the gift of the incarnation.

And the pentecostal theological and spiritual tradition is very taken with the second sending, convinced that it was not only a defining moment in the early life of the church but rather that it is necessarily defining for each Christian and for the church of each generation. It is a perspective that is inclined to highlight the phenomenal line toward the conclusion of the Gospel of Luke, the words of Jesus (Lk 24:49) who urges his disciples to wait until they were "clothed with power from on high." Thus it follows—for those within the holiness and pentecostal tradition—that even as the church experienced the incarnation and the death, resurrection, and ascension of Christ the church also, as a distinct experience, knows the gift of the Spirit. The second is the essential complement to the first. And yet, and this is the critical piece, they are still distinct and not merged. Thus the church responds to two sendings and knows the grace of two distinct experiences.

Before we focus on the implications of the second sending, we mustn't miss the pivotal affirmation that the second is anchored in the first, a complement to the first. While there are two sendings, the second is anchored in the first and the second sending is the complement to the first. Furthermore, it fulfills the first, that "God sent his Son." Thus the two are distinct, but they need to be viewed in tandem.

The second sending is equally essential to the first. There is no experience of Christ that is not mediated by the Spirit; all we know of Christ, including a knowledge of Christ's love, is granted to the church by the Spirit. And more, even though this experience of the Spirit is grounded in the life of the church and complemented by the witness of the Scriptures, the experience is immediate—drawing God's people, collectively and individually, into the very presence of Christ. As I stressed in the chapter on Luke–Acts, the ascension and Pentecost are distinct but inseparable. The Spirit is sent—given—that through this gift, the church is empowered to abide in the Son. The Spirit is sent so that the church abides in the love of Christ (see Rom 5:5). Consider the even more explicit language of 1 John 4:13: "By this we know that we abide in him and he in us, because he has given us of his Spirit." In and through the Spirit, the gift from God, the church is drawn into fellowship with Christ.

The *Filioque* Clause

Surely this "distinct but inseparable" perspective is what should inform the historic debate over the *filioque* clause in the Western version of the Nicene Creed. The Creed reads as follows:

. . . Holy Spirit, the Lord, the giver of life,
who proceeds from the Father *and the Son*,
who with the Father and the Son is adored and glorified.

Starting in and around the sixth century, churches in the west were using a version of the creed that included the slight addition— "and the Son"—very specifically to protect what was then viewed as an indispensable understanding of the unity of the Trinity and the Christological character of the ministry of the Spirit.

The debate centers around the question, who gives or who sends the Spirit? Is it the Father, as seems to be suggested by Acts 11:16-17 and John 14:26. Or is it the Son who sends the Spirit, as suggested John 16:7?

The Eastern church has always vigorously protested this addition, viewing this revision as a threat to the unity and character of the Trinity. The protest is understandable in the sense that the Creed, once given, is, well, given. The church is not free to revise or amend the ancient creeds. And yet surely a way forward can be found in stressing the following: yes, there is only one Father, who is the source of all things and who is truly the one from whom the Spirit proceeds. But, and this is crucial, the Spirit is sent through the Son so that the Spirit comes to the world and the church from the Father and the Son, but only in the sense that the only Spirit we know is the Spirit whose coming arises from and is known through the grace of the work of Christ—crucified, risen, and ascended. What we are seeking, both East and West, is an understanding of the Spirit that affirms this: the Spirit is very God of very God, the Father is the source of all things, and all of God's work in the world is in and through the Son. The West added the *filioque* clause to protect the meaning of the Trinity; the East viewed this addition as actually undermining the meaning of the Trinity. The question is whether, while disagreeing on whether the clause should or should not have been added, we can at least agree on this: any understanding we have of the Spirit is that the Spirit has been given by the Father through the Son and that the only Spirit we know is the Spirit whose work in our lives, in the church, and in the world is the Spirit who comes in the name of Christ.

But then we need to stress the following. While the two sendings are inseparable, they *are* distinct; while all we know of Christ is mediated by the Spirit, the sending of the Spirit is a distinct act or sending in its own right and thus it is a distinct experience in its own right, the experience of the gracious filling of the Spirit. And thus the pentecostal and holiness traditions have consistently emphasized the value if not the actual need for a distinct experience of the Spirit as a critical dimension of Christian initiation and as a vital dynamic of the on-going growth of the church and the individual Christian.

Experience matters. As noted, for this tradition, experience matters. There is also no doubt that this entire mystical and charismatic theological and spiritual tradition has particularly given significance to experience—most notably, the immediate experience of the Spirit—an experience of supernatural grace, experience that cannot be attributed to natural causes but only to the Spirit. The church is a people who have been unequivocally graced by the Spirit. And here is where there is continuity between the charismatic and pentecostal movements of recent decades and this more ancient and historic mystical movement which had such currency prior to the Protestant Reformation and with the sixteenth century Catholic Reformers.

To use the language of the Ignatian tradition, it is a "consolation without previous cause." Furthermore, this consolation—this experience of the Spirit—is felt. It is an *affective* awareness. This experience of God, of the Spirit, is not some secondary or superficial dimension to the life of the church. To the contrary, as Lesslie Newbigin rightly notes, "the gift of the Holy Spirit [is] an event which can be unmistakably recognized . . . and the determinative and decisive thing by which the Church is constituted." Newbigin makes this point as the conclusion to a series of reflections on the vital place of religious experience as the expression of the Spirit in the life of the Christian and the life of the church.

The crucial or critical matter to appreciate is that the experience—the affective awareness, the heartfelt knowledge—is very specifically of God's very self. And the ancient mystics and the contemporary charismatic would suggest to us that this is not some unusual or perhaps more specifically elitist experience reserved for a few but rather the actual and very meaning of Christian existence. It thus shapes the ordinary and mundane contours and elements of each individual life and the life of each congregation of Christian believers.

In speaking of the ordinary, we are not discounting the place of ecstasy or of the unusual or the spontaneous. Yet we should not assume that the experience of the Spirit means that routines, rituals, and the rhythms of daily life, indeed in the very ordinariness of lived experience—in the quotidian of our lives—are dismissed. The Spirit must be found and known in the ordinary; if it is not found here—in the ordinary—it will not ultimately be transformative.

So many charismatic and pentecostal perspectives imply or assume that the Holy Spirit is a special superhuman power and wisdom—not found in teaching and study, not found through intentional practice. Some actually view discipline, study, and intentional practice as somehow a threat to the knowledge of the Spirit. But whereas the books of Luke and Acts do highlight the numinous and the extra-ordinary, it is also evident that the experience of the Spirit is basic and foundational to the life of the church, and that it finds expression in the routines of the church—thus, Acts 2:42—what did the "spirit baptized" church do? They devoted themselves to the apostles teaching and the breaking of bread, to the fellowship and the prayers. Furthermore, the apostle Paul seems to indicate that the essence of the pentecostal experience is not charismata—whether that be healings, tongues-speaking, or ecstatic experience—but rather the fruit of the Spirit (Gal 5:22), which then is a means by which the Spirit graces ordinary Christian community. I am not for a moment in these observations minimizing the spontaneous or the miraculous or the extra-ordinary; I am merely indicating that these are not the *essence* of the Spirit-filled life. I am not saying that they are of a former "dispensation." Rather, I am stressing that the heart of the Spirit-filled life is an immediate awareness of the presence of Christ, and the fruit or evidence of that awareness is the quality of human existence that is the fruit of living "in Christ" in gracious community.

The essence of the pentecostal awareness is not good feelings as an end in themselves, but rather two things, the knowledge of Christ and the transforming work of grace. The Spirit's work, in other words, is not to infantilize us but to foster our capacity for maturity in Christ. The work of the Spirit does not cancel out clear thought and depth of intellectual conviction; it does not eliminate the need to lean into the weight of the Christian tradition and learning.

Thus there is great wisdom in viewing the contemporary charismatic movement as in direct continuity with the mystical traditions in the history of the church. For the mystics always knew and affirmed that not all experience is authentically of the Spirit, no matter how ecstatic or wonderful the experience may have been. They stressed the need for discernment, for testing and proving and verifying that indeed an experience "of the spirit" is very truly an experience of the Spirit of God. In the language of 1 Thessalonians 5:19, we do not quench the Spirit. We can and must lift up our hearts eager to know the grace of the Spirit, engaging our deepest sensibilities in a yearning to know the unmediated grace and presence of the Spirit in our lives. But we must also be astute, discerning, and capable of testing everything (1 Thess 5:21).

Further, the mystical tradition has always recognized that the Spirit often works in our lives in a manner that is deep, quiet, and not always emotionally satisfying. John of the Cross could speak of the "dark night," for example. And this is not a suggestion that God is not as present to the Christian but rather that the deep work of God may often come to us in times of winter silence, even darkness. This darkness or quietness is not a signal that something is wrong but rather that the work of the Spirit in our lives and in our midst happens in times of joyful engagement but also in times of quiet, when the heart is still, perhaps even in times of emotional desolation or darkness. In other words, all of us—the Pentecostal included—need to affirm a simple but powerful observation: we do not equate the work of the Spirit with height of emotional expression.

And yet the bottom line remains: the genius of the pentecostal vision is that we have an unmediated experience, however ecstatic or unusual or ordinary, that cannot be attributed to any other source than God's very self, graciously offered and given and known. And the point is that this not something unique and thus open to a few, but rather that this experience of the spirit is the birthright of every Christian. Thus we have Karl Rahner's justly famous observation that the devout Christian of the future will be a mystic who has experienced the other, the transcendent, or he or she will not be a Christian at all. And in the warp and woof of daily experience, what defines us is not deep thoughts or heroic actions but a powerful contentment, a delight in God and in the love of God.

It also means that we take experience seriously and allow our experience of the Spirit to inform our theological vision of life, of the church, and of the world. We can ask the question, what is the Spirit doing and how is the Spirit present and teaching us, guiding us? Those of a more Wesleyan perspective have always insisted that experience is a source for theology. And it is interesting to see contemporary feminist theologians also insist that perhaps we can actually begin with the Spirit when we articulate our understanding of the Triune God. In other words, classic approaches to reflection on the Trinity have typically begun with the Father, then considered person and work of the Son and, then and only then, the work of the Spirit. This has for many been the standard structure for systematic theology in theological schools—often even, as it was in my formation, articulated as Theology I, II, and III, with Theology III, of course, being the course where we finally considered pneumatology, the theology of the Holy Spirit. But some, such as Elizabeth A. Johnson, suggest that the early church came to an understanding of God through an experience of the salvation of God, and that our understanding of the Trinity might then, appropriately, actually *begin* with a consideration of the work of the Spirit. The main point I am making here is that experience matters and that with discernment, of course, it is indeed a source for theological and ethical reflection. We understand God by attending to the ways of God, which is but another way of saying, by attending to the ways of the Spirit. And this also means that we attend to those voices that have learned to draw on experience for theological reflection. It means that we can rightly speak of the mystics as doctors of the church—theological sources for whom their primary data was their experience: Bernard of Clairvaux, Teresa of Avila, John of the Cross, and others.

Creation, ecology, and the brooding Spirit. The theological foundations for the pentecostal vision of divine grace also necessarily reference not only the experience of the individual Christian and the church but also the work of the Spirit in the created order. That is, a dynamic and more comprehensive theology of the Spirit will include and be grounded in a theology of creation. There is a powerful counterpoint between Genesis 1 and Romans 8. The Spirit at creation hovers over the void and the darkness, and out of darkness and void brings light and life. This same Spirit is referenced in Romans 8, groaning, yearning, and longing for the healing of all things.

Few have witnessed to this connection as brilliantly as the English Jesuit poet, Gerard Manley Hopkins. He is a true sacramentalist when he opens what is for many the favorite of his poems with this line: "The world is charged with the grandeur of God." But then, he ends this same poem with these exquisite words:

Oh, morning, at the brown brink eastward, springs—
Because the Holy Ghost over the bent
World broods with warm breast and with ah! bright wings.

This is a reminder to us that our pneumatology, our theology of the Spirit, can and must incorporate a delight in beauty and an appreciation for the vital importance of the created order. First, our engagement with the Spirit leads to a deep appreciation for and commitment to beauty. As Hans Urs von Balthasar has stressed, beauty is indispensable to life; beauty is the very means by which God is known and the Spirit is present to us. Thus the artists in our midst are crucial pentecostal vangards, gifts (charismata) of the Spirit, who enable the church and the world to know the beauty, holiness, and love of the Creator.

Artists thus value the reference to Bezalel, who played a key role in the building of the tabernacle, as described in Exodus 31:2-5:

See, I have called by name Bezalel son of Uri son of Hur, of the tribe of Judah: and I have filled him with divine spirit, with ability, intelligence, and knowledge in every kind of craft, to devise artistic designs, to work in gold, silver, and bronze, in cutting stones for setting, and in carving wood, in every kind of craft.

And second, it means that if we are "in the Spirit," we will attend to those who call us to seek the healing of creation—prophets, advocates, environmentally attentive scientists. They too are agents of the Spirit, charismatic gifts and participants in the gracious purposes of God in the world.

WORD AND SACRAMENT REMAIN

When we speak of the immediacy of the Spirit—of how as the church, we lean into and depend on the gracious power of the Spirit consciously and deliberately—this does not for a moment diminish or discount the place of the sacraments or the Scriptures in the life of the church. In all that follows, we can and must continue to assume that God is present to and gracing the church through Word and sacrament. We make disciples baptizing and teaching them (Mt 28:18-20); the early church devoted themselves to the apostles teaching and "breaking of bread" (Acts 2:42). We can embrace a full and dynamic appreciation of the Spirit in the life of the church without in any way diminishing the critical role of the Scriptures—read and preached—and the fundamental rites of baptism and the Lord's Supper. Word and sacrament are an indispensable means by which the Spirit graces the church, the individual Christian, and indeed the world. More, they are the very means by which the Spirit is present to the church, graces the church, and empowers and equips the church to be the church. It is no overstatement that it grieves the Holy Spirit when we neglect the Scriptures or the sacraments.

In many evangelical circles, it is not uncommon to hear a growing emphasis on the need for discipleship and spiritual formation. Appropriately so; this is so very important. And often this is linked to the need for the church to have, as it is often put, a "fresh" experience of the Spirit. While this is, of course, a good thing and a timely emphasis, it needs at the very least to reference if not actually lead to a renewed emphasis on teaching and learning, on the ministry of the

Word, and then, also, on the sacramental rites of the church. The most fundamental means by which the Spirit does the Spirit's work of transformation in the life of the church is through Word and sacrament. These, together, are foundational.

But more, what needs to also be stressed is that in our very liturgies we should make it abundantly clear that the operative agent in both Word and sacrament is the Spirit. That is, in our worship, it should be clear—evident and obvious—that both Word and sacrament are supremely charismatic events, means and moments wherein the Spirit of the Living God is present to the world. Everything that follows in what I am about to stress in this chapter assumes Word and sacrament as precisely the means of divine grace, means by which the Spirit does what the Spirit was sent by the Father, through the Son, to do. Indeed, I would go further: we are going to speak of the immediacy of the Spirit in the life of the church, but we can only truly do so if and as both Word and sacrament are fully informing, animating, and grounding the life of the church. We are not truly pentecostal, in other words, unless we are sacramental, and we are not truly a people who live in the fullness of the Spirit if we are not a people who live by and are feeding on the Word.

Without Word and sacrament, "charismatic" worship descends to mere sentimentality, focused on human felt need, as often as not emotional need. Thus we should have a concern with what might be called the "pentecostalization" of evangelical worship events—the grand stage, the manipulation of emotion, the removal of the table (with the implied downplaying of the sacraments), the removal of the pulpit—replaced by the lectern at best and the chair by the café-bistro table at worse (for the pastor's friendly chat)—so that the visual centerpiece of worship is not the table or the pulpit but the drum set. Yes, all Christian communities surely need to know the very thing that the mystical and pentecostal tradition has consistently affirmed: the immediacy of the Spirit in the life of the Christian and the life of the church. But it is not at the expense of either the authority of the Word and of preaching or the vital and defining place of the sacrament. Rather it is necessarily the case that the experience of the Spirit is both the complement to and the very means by which Word and sacrament are present to the church.

And yet having stressed the importance and priority of both Word and sacrament, we can still and we must affirm that there is a witness in the New Testament to something without doubt experienced often in the life of the church that we can and must speak of as "unmediated grace." We can and need to speak of the immediate gift of the Spirit to the Christian and to the church, a gift that is experienced as divine grace, empowerment, illumination, and comfort. Our experience of the Spirit is not something in the background but rather, a dynamic experience of God's grace that informs—well, a better word is *animates*—the life of the Christian and the life of the church.

BEING INTENTIONAL: LEARNING TO LIVE "IN THE SPIRIT"

The bottom line is that if we are truly pentecostal, we will have a theology of the Holy Spirit that will inform and infuse the life of the ordinary Christian—sufficiently so that the typical Christian believer will know what it means to live in dynamic fellowship with the Spirit, living not as a naturalist, but with an awareness of transcendent presence in life, work, and relationships.

This will be evident in a number of ways.

Surprises. If we are pentecostal, we are open to surprises. I will address the need for intentionality below, but we must begin with this affirmation: the Spirit cannot be controlled, manipulated, or commodified. Simon Chan observes that while the downside of the pentecostal tradition includes a disparagement of routine, ritual, and said prayers, the counter to this is that those of us who are more comfortable in ordered and intentionally structured settings and liturgies need to affirm that the Spirit is the Spirit and more than able to bypass the program and be present in our lives in ways that confound our plans and procedures.

We are inclined to be open to the work of the Spirit as long as the Spirit follows the rules—learns the prayer book; respects our liturgies; agrees with our hermeneutic and thus our reading of Holy Scripture; and affirms our structures of good governance. But the witness of the New Testament suggests otherwise: however important it is that we turn to our prayer books, learn to read Scripture with a mature hermeneutic, and attend to the wisdom of good administrative structures, the Spirit is "free." That is, the Spirit is able and willing and insistent on bypassing all of this and surprising us. And this happens as a subtle reminder that ultimately all is from the Spirit.

The anointing of the sick. Second, we must speak of the grace of anointing the sick and actually expecting them to know the healing grace of the Spirit. The ministry of anointing should never be viewed as antithetical to the good work of medicine, neither should it be framed in a way that discounts the reality of suffering in the world, in the church, and in the life of the Christian. We can and must affirm the place of the medical profession in care of body and soul; this work is no less the work of God and the healing grace of the Spirit than the laying on of hands. Further, we can and must affirm that we are called to suffer with Christ (Rom 8:17), and that much of the grace of the Spirit is precisely this empowerment to carry the weight of the world.

And yet the pentecostal tradition affirms, and rightly, the distinctive place of the church in the laying on of hands—the anointing of the sick—with the expectation that they will know the sustaining and healing grace of the Spirit. I use the word *expectation* intentionally, suggesting that while we do not presume, we do actually anticipate that the Spirit of God would intervene in our broken and fragmented world—in our bodies, in our communities, between peoples, in ways that could only be accredited to the intervention of the Spirit of God.

Discernment (and prophecies). If we stand within the ancient mystical tradition and the more recent pentecostal witness to the work of the Spirit, we will affirm that there is indeed the possibility of an immediate connection to the Spirit for the critical choices we are called to make. We will be attentive to how the Spirit is now, in real time, giving direction and insight to the church.

When the church is wrestling with a significant decision on ethical matters, for example, the Evangelical will appeal to Scripture and consider what the Bible says we should do on this or that or the other. And if Evangelicals disagree on something, they will typically appeal to the Bible and see who has the most verses supporting their position. The sacramental Christian would typically appeal to the historic tradition.

But the pentecostal principle would suggest that we can also ask, "What is the Spirit saying to the church, in our time and place?" This does not necessarily mean that Scripture and tradition do not matter to the mystic or the Pentecostal. Rather, it does mean that the immediate witness of the Spirit is or at least can be a very significant factor in our discernment. When faced with a key issue or decision, in other words, we would ask, "How is the Spirit taking the ancient text, as the baseline for all that we consider, and how does the church's tradition finding expression today through the work of the Spirit?" It means that the experience of the Spirit is a dynamic source for guidance and discernment, along with Scripture (evangelical) and tradition (sacramental).

But also, those within the charismatic and pentecostal traditions typically affirm the possibility of a prophetic word: an individual within the community, perhaps, has a "word" from God for the community. If this word is truly from God, it will be consistent with and in continuity with Scripture and tradition. The canon is closed. But it will still be a new word—from God, through a prophetic utterance—signaling how the church today is being called to live in a way that is faithful to the gospel. Discernment is still required, always. And yet the mystical and pentecostal traditions affirm the potential for this kind of immediacy—Christ, through the work of the Spirit, speaking to the church today.

The church—a Pentecostal perspective. If we are truly pentecostal in our sensibilities, the pentecostal principle will inform our understanding of the church and how the church is governed in several ways. First, the Spirit is an ecumenical spirit; if we are in the Spirit, we are committed to working with and fostering the unity of the church universal. Pentecostal sectarianism is an oxymoron. The Spirit is a unifying agent, the mothering presence of God that unites the children of God. The Day of Pentecost speaks not only of the outpouring of the Spirit but also of the formation of the church. And there is only one church and thus there is no surprise that the Scriptures call the church to make "every effort to maintain the unity of the Spirit in the bond of peace" (Eph 4:3).

Second, we recognize that the mission of the church—witnessing in word and deed to the reign of Christ—will be explicitly and intentionally done in the power of the Spirit. We will welcome the diverse ways in which men and women are called of the Spirit into mission and we will welcome the signs that are evidence of the Spirit's work, recognizing that mission is not ultimately about our accomplishments, but rather it is about God. Thus we will come up against those moments, those events, those experiences, in mission, that can only be attributed to God's intervention in our lives, in our churches, and in our world.

And third, if we are truly pentecostal, we will appreciate that in our governance, in the way that the church is organized and structured, there will be a stream of witness by the Spirit to and within and from the church that bypasses our systems of governance. Karl Rahner speaks of a dynamic and healthy tension between the institutional church and the charismatic church. He rightly insists that neither is a threat to the other; they mutually reinforce and strengthen each other. The Spirit does work through those who have official roles or responsibilities in the church (the clergy, for example). And good governance matters. And yet Rahner observes that the New Testament witnesses to a variety of charisms, gifts, that may or may not be exercised through the church's official ministry. Rahner, very much in sync with the mystical tradition at this point, observes that this is a work of the Spirit that complements the work of the Spirit through the teaching and sacramental offices of the church.

And finally, I think of the observation that New Testament scholar Gordon Fee made numerous times to anyone who would listen—evidence of his own pentecostal roots but also his capacity to read the Scriptures through the lens of Pentecost: the basis for ministry in the life of the church is not gender but the calling of the Spirit. And the Spirit clearly calls women every bit as much as the Spirit calls men. In the words of Acts 2:17, "your sons and your daughters shall prophesy."

Beyond this, the pentecostal perspective would insist that the basis for ministry and for ordination is not that one is learned but called, not that one has graduate theological formation but rather than one has a distinctive anointing that gives evidence of this calling. We might, of course, insist that it is not either/or; one can be both learned and called. But the pentecostal appreciation would stress that it is the Spirit's anointing that ultimately matters most.

Prayer. The pentecostal principle undergirds a particular appreciation of prayer, that in prayer we foster the capacity for immediacy—for the cultivation of affective prayer, for the inner orientation that leans into a conscious awareness of the presence of God, specifically the love of God. It is to speak of and experience prayer as not only talking to God but actually encountering the ineffable presence of God and to find in God one's true home. Then we live in the world—in our relationships and our work—from this encounter with God. The whole of the Christian experience is then lived from this place, from this way of being, which then informs everyday life. And this transformed life in the world *must* follow: the ineffable experience only has currency if it then in turn fosters the capacity for joy in the midst of daily life.

Tongues-speaking. For many within the charismatic movement, tongues-speaking has been regarded as a defining evidence of an experience of the Spirit. There is a debate whether tongues-speaking is crucial evidence—that is, an essential expression of the life of the Spirit in the life of the individual Christian and the church. In my estimation, it is not essential. And yet, what it does speak to is an appreciation within the mystical and pentecostal movement and tradition that indeed an intimate knowledge of the Spirit may include ecstatic experience. In other words, many within this stream of the Christian movement have had a significant experience of the intimacy and immediacy of the Spirit that was and is expressed in *glossolalia*, or tongues-speaking. While in itself not essential, it is one means by which this immediacy of the Spirit is known. And crucially, the bottom line is not whether the immediate experience of the Spirit leads to tongues-speaking, but whether it is evident in the fruit of the Spirit—love, joy, and peace.

FOSTERING INTENTIONALITY

This brings us back to where I opened this chapter, the reference to the closing verses of Galatians where the apostle, through a set of observations and invitations calls his readers to—if we take all of these references as a whole—a life of "living in the Spirit." A similar observation could be made regarding a parallel list of imperatives found towards the end of another Pauline letter, Ephesians. Both call for intentionality when it comes to the response of the Christian and of the church to the work of the Spirit.

The book of Ephesians has three distinct references to this very call to intentionality.

Ephesians 3:16 is a call and invitation to be strengthened in one's inner being by the Spirit. This is clearly a call to a more conscious and intentional awareness of the Spirit's empowerment, which the Scriptures at this point link to an intimate knowledge of God's love (echoing Rom 5:5).

Ephesians 5:18 is an exhortation to be filled with the Spirit, a filling that will be reflected in song and thanksgiving, or perhaps better put, hearts filled with thanksgiving that then in turn find expression in song. Paul urges the church to be filled with the Spirit, and Paul urges the church to sing. Steven R. Guthrie makes the observation that the two should perhaps indeed be linked. As those who are being filled by the Spirit, we are called to speak to one another in songs, hymns, and spiritual songs—singing, making music, giving thanks—suggesting, Guthrie observes, that through our singing we enact the new community, in the Spirit, to which we are called, singing together with one voice. I would add that the act of singing together not only brings us together but is also the vital means by which we lift up our hearts, open our hearts to God and to the Spirit. Thus it would be said that our song is both a response to the gift of the Spirit—seemingly an essential response—and further, it is the very means by which we open our hearts up to the gracious work of the Spirit in our midst.

Thus Christian worship includes exuberant song, the careful reading and consideration of the Scriptures, and the Table. All three.

And then we have Ephesians 6:18 with the call to prayer, but specifically prayer in the Spirit: "Pray in the Spirit at all times in every prayer and supplication."

The conclusion we come to is quite simple: the Christian life is lived intentionally in the Spirit. And it makes sense that this intentionality be reflected in, at the very least, two significant actions of the church when it comes to initiation into the Christian life. First, the rite of initiation would include *chrismation*, something I will speak to more fully in the conclusion of this book. And second, catechesis—the introduction and formation into the Christian faith—would actually include teaching, instruction, on how to live in the Spirit. And for that, we lean into the ancient mystical tradition and the experience of the more contemporary pentecostal and charismatic movements of the last century.

CONCLUSION

Some Observations and a Case Study

In conclusion, consider three observations and a case study.

CHRISTIAN COMMUNITY

First, it needs to be stressed that the grace of God is always located within Christian community. The Spirit, the Word, and the sacramental life of the church are all housed within a community that is demarcated by love and committed to mission in the world. Thus the work of the Spirit finds expression within the dynamics of Christian fellowship; the Word is spoken and heard within a living congregation; and the sacraments are, of course, fundamentally and essentially acts of the community within community.

And thus those of an evangelical, sacramental, and pentecostal persuasion need to attend to the wisdom and insights of those for whom the essence of the church is its life in community, the orientation that the community is itself a vehicle of or means of the grace of God. Yes, of course, the community is grace and a means of grace if it is a community of the Word, of the Table, and of the fellowship of the Spirit. And yet this caveat does not for a moment discount the need to attend to the communal dynamics of the grace of God.

THE GREAT FESTIVALS

Second, I wonder if we can speak of three great festivals in the life of the church that in a way correspond to the three perspectives of grace—evangelical, sacramental, and pentecostal.

Why not approach Advent–Christmas–Epiphany as that season of the year when we learn to lean into the wonder of the incarnation and grow in our appreciation of the sacramental means of grace? God became flesh; we celebrate the deep power of this physicality in the communication of the grace of God.

To approach the season of Lent through till Holy Week, including Good Friday and Easter Sunday, as a rich time of the year when we can enter intentionally into the Scriptures—re-learning and re-appropriating the Word to which we respond penitentially, especially through Lent. Perhaps we can view Lent as a season when other sources—media for example—are set aside for an extended immersion in the Scriptures all leading up to the celebration of Christ and Christ crucified and risen and of the gospel proclaimed.

And then also, could we see the time between Ascension Day and Pentecost, from the fortieth until the fiftieth day after Easter, a ten day window in the calendar, as the occasion and opportunity to enter afresh into the gift of the Spirit? Pentecost Sunday, then, would have similar weight to the celebrations we have for Advent–Christmas. We would start with Ascension Day and then move to the Sunday after for a full appreciation of the wonder that Christ is at the right hand of God. Then after a week of waiting and anticipation, we would gather for a renewed celebration of and appropriation of the gift of the Spirit on the Day of Pentecost.

Why not use these three festivals to give focused attention to the three key expressions of the grace of the ascended Christ in the life of the church?

LITURGICAL SPACE

Third, it is essential to remember that we speak volumes by the design of liturgical space and how we engage that space. Built and designed space is not a matter of theological neutrality. And this has implications for how we live out the conviction that we are going to be evangelical, sacramental, and pentecostal.

The evangelical tradition, with its emphasis on the Word, has insisted that the priority of the Word is evident in the distinct priority given to the pulpit, the representation of the Word proclaimed, placing it visually front and center. Older Protestant and evangelical churches would sometimes have very large pulpits. The Communion table, typically used only occasionally, once a month in some churches, would be very obviously lower, perhaps on the lower level. No one attending worship in such a church would doubt the priority of the Word.

Sacramental traditions in contrast have the Table front and center. There will be a podium or lectern and perhaps even a preaching pulpit up front, but these will very obviously be to one side. The distinct visual center of the worship will be the Table, even spoken of as an altar in some settings, as the obvious focus of attention. If for the Evangelical, the high point of Worship is the preaching of the Scriptures, for the sacramental Christian it is clearly the Table and the celebration of the Eucharist.

And it is very interesting to see how liturgical and worship furnishings have evolved over the last number of years. The growing strength of the pentecostal and charismatic movement and its influence in evangelical churches, in particular, has meant a number of things. First, the pulpit is typically gone and replaced by a very portable lectern. In some cases, there is literally no representation of the preached Word. Even the lectern has been replaced by the bistro table and bar stool, while the equivalent of the sermon has become a more casual chat, downplaying almost intentionally the authority of the Scriptures in an attempt to make the Word more accessible. As often as not, the communion table, which for my upbringing was always viewed an important item of furniture even when not being used, has been removed. And now what is front and center—with the pulpit and the communion table gone—is, I say this without any exaggeration, the drum set. This pattern is ubiquitous.

Is there a better way forward that reflects an appreciation for the power of space and the visual expressions of our theological convictions?

Why not actually make it clear that this is a congregation that affirms both Word and sacrament, evident in a pulpit that clearly signals that something sacred and of utmost significance happens when the Scriptures are opened and read and proclaimed? We can make evident that the celebration of the Lord's Supper is the essential counterpart to the Word in this: the Table is not lower or off to one side but on the same level as the pulpit, signaling that with the Word and as the complement to the Word, this congregation knows the grace of the ascended Christ. The front and center of Christian worship, then, would be Word and Table, side by side, each given equal weight as the counterpart of the other.

But how do we represent the presence and grace of the Holy Spirit in our worship? The ideal, of course, would be to signal somehow that the Spirit hovers over and infuses all of our worship, drawing our attention to the risen and ascended Christ. The cross, representing Christ, is ideally clearly that which defines this as a Christ event. But is there a way to re-present the convictions this congregation has about the ministry of the Holy Spirit?

One example might be that of the huge, stunning glass sculpture that hangs above the high altar at the Cathedral of St. Mary of the Assumption in San Francisco that re-presents the outpouring and presence of the Holy Spirit in worship. Or perhaps another option would be liturgical banners could be designed and hung to signal that every aspect and dimension of the liturgical is prompted by and guided by the presence of the Holy Spirit.

The main point here is that the visual dimensions of worship complement the words spoken and the prayers offered. If a church is truly evangelical, it will be evident in that what we see in worship affirms the vital place of and the authority of the Scriptures and more, the particular place of preaching in the church's worship.

If we are truly sacramental, no one will doubt this when they enter into our worship space. We will signal that we are here as a baptized people, perhaps with the baptismal pool located near the entry to the sanctuary—actually an ancient practice as is evident in fifth century churches, notably in Ravenna, Italy. And even when the Lord's Supper is not being celebrated, the Table will always be there and visible as a continual reminder that Christ reveals himself to his people at the Table.

And if we are leaning into and depending on the ministry of the Holy Spirit, this too will be signaled; as worshipers, we would know that this is a venue for worship where the theological convictions regarding the Spirit are evident in both the practice and experience of worship in this church.

CHRISTIAN INITIATION

Finally, I offer the following a case study: if we are evangelical, sacramental, and pentecostal, what would Christian initiation look like? The words of Acts 2:38-42 almost provide us with just such a full-orbed model, one might say, of the process of Christian initiation. In response to Peter's sermon on the day of Pentecost, Peter and the other apostles are asked, "What shall we do?" And the response was simply this: "Repent, and be baptized every one of you in the name of Jesus Christ so that your sins may be forgiven; and you will receive the gift of the Holy Spirit" (Acts 2:38). And then, we read in Acts 2:42, "they devoted themselves to the apostles' teaching and fellowship, to the breaking of bread and the prayers."

Perhaps then, working with Acts 2 in light of the words of Jesus at the conclusion of the book of Matthew, we would recognize that Christian initiation includes, at the very least, three key elements. First, there would be high focus on the Scriptures, studied and preached, to the end of fostering alignment—repentance as alignment—with the in-breaking of the reign of Christ. This might be an extended process leading up to baptism and initiation. But the main point is that the focus would be the teachings of the prophets and the apostles, allowing Christ to speak through the Word to call a potential follower to himself. And we would appreciate the ancient practice of seeing Lent as essentially a season of penitential preparation for one's baptism, and we would see conversion as entering into the penitential way. Bible study would be an essential part of the coming to faith. The proclamation of the Scriptures would be taken as an integral part of the way that God calls someone to faith in Christ. And a new Christian would be taught the basics of how to read and engage the Scriptures.

Second, there would be an invitation to baptism, seeing water baptism as a pivotal embodiment of one's emerging interior faith. Thus one's baptism is not only the focal point of Christian initiation but also the avenue through which one enters into a full sacramental experience. Some traditions might reserve the Lord's Supper for those who have been baptized; others might see the Lord's Supper as a vital means by which Christ is drawing people to himself. Either way, a sacramental perspective on Christian initiation would affirm the central place of baptism in the process and the simple reality that initiation is always initiation not into a privatized faith but a shared faith that finds expression in a sacramental community.

And then, third, we would also speak of *chrismation*—anointing with oil—representing the intentional appropriation of the gift of the Spirit, and a strong declaration that one cannot live the Christian life except by the grace of the Spirit. It would be abundantly clear that people are only truly initiated into the faith when they engage the Scriptures through biblical preaching and teaching, when they are baptized and when, furthermore, they know the anointing of the Spirit. The premise here is simple: one cannot live the Christian life until and unless one knows how to walk in the Spirit. Thus *chrismation*—the anointing with oil and the prayer for the reception of the gift of the Spirit—would be viewed as integral to the process of coming to faith in Christ and being initiated into the Christian journey. This would seem to be the pattern of the apostle himself who, we read in Acts 19, came to Ephesus and initiated those there into the Christian faith. Instruction was followed by baptism. And then, we read, Paul laid hands on them and the Holy Spirit came upon them (Acts 19:6).

A service of baptism, therefore, would have each of these distinctive elements. The Word would come early in the service, signaling that baptism is in response to the Word preached. Why not actually have the baptismal candidates seated to hear the word that is given to them but also to all whose baptismal vows are being renewed that day. And then, following the water baptism there would be a chrismation with the laying on of hands. The elders of the church community would lay hands on those who have been baptized, anointing them with oil, with the prayer that each would receive the gift of the Spirit. And then they would be formally welcomed into the faith community.

By making all three explicit as part of the very process of initiation into the Christian faith, we increase the possibility that the new Christian will not only come to faith but grow in faith—not only enter into the Christian life but mature as a one who knows how to appropriate the fullness of divine grace, in all the ways that it is available to each one of us. This new Christian would very much be a person of the Scriptures—knowing how to study, read, and pray the Scriptures and how to participate in a community that is formed by the preaching of the Word.

The new Christian would recognize the vital place of the Lord's Supper, within Christian community, as an essential means by which the Christian meets God, walks with God, grows in faith, and lives in Christian community.

And, of course, the new Christian would know what it means to live in the Spirit, walk in the Spirit, be guided by the Spirit, and bear the fruit of the Spirit.

In other words, the Christian would be evangelical, sacramental, and pentecostal. And the evidence of such would be that they live with a deep and resilient joy, the fruit of a life lived in dynamic union with the ascended Christ.

NOTES

INTRODUCTION

3　*One of the most important books on ecclesiology*: Lesslie Newbigin, *The Household of God* (London: SCM Press, 1953).

　　Experienced effects: Ibid., 30.

　　The church is: Ibid.

4　*Christological concentration*: Michael Wecker, *What Happens in Holy Communion?*, trans. John F. Hoffmeyer (Grand Rapids: Eerdmans, 2000), 174.

3 THE GRACE OF GOD:
EVANGELICAL, SACRAMENTAL, AND PENTECOSTAL

39　*To experience grace*: Christian Wiman, *My Bright Abyss: Meditation of a Modern Believer* (New York: Farrar, Straus, and Giroux, 2013), 4.

42　*The sacraments and the Spirit*: John Calvin, *Institutes of the Christian Religion, a New Translation by Henry Beveridge* (Edinburgh: Calvin Translation Society, 1845), 4.19.9.

45　*The role of sacraments*: Ibid., 4.14.1.

46　*First, we must understand*: Ibid., 3.1.1.

47　*Wesley's sermons*: John Wesley, "Sermon 10" and "Sermon 11," http://wesley.nnu.edu/john-wesley/the-sermons-of-john-wesley-1872

-edition/sermon-10-the-witness-of-the-spirit-discourse-one; and http://wesley.nnu.edu/john-wesley/the-sermons-of-john-wesley-1872 -edition/sermon-11-the-witness-of-the-spirit-discourse-two.

48 Sermon 107, "On God's Vineyard," I.1 (quoting Ps 119:105), *The Bicentennial Edition of The Works of John Wesley* (Nashville: Abingdon, 1984–), 3:504; and "Short History of Methodism," *Works* [BE], 9:369.

   How Wesley uses Scripture: Scott J. Jones, *John Wesley's Conception and Use of Scripture* (Nashville: Abingdon Press, 1995), 217-22.

49 *The Duty of Constant Communion*: John Wesley, "The Duty of Constant Communion," Sermon 101, http://wesley.nnu.edu/john-wesley/the -sermons-of-john-wesley-1872-edition/sermon-101-the-duty-of -constant-communion.

   A challenge for Wesley scholars: See for example Ted A. Campbell, "Conversion and Baptism in Wesleyan Spirituality," in *Conversion in the Wesleyan Tradition*, ed. Kenneth J. Collins and John H. Tyson (Abingdon, 2001), 160-74. Campbell observes that Wesley's juxtaposition of the sacramental and the evangelical has "posed very difficult issues for the interpretation of Wesleyan theology and spirituality." Ibid., 160.

50 *Strangely warmed*: A reference to how Wesley speaks of his experience in 1738, to the heartfelt knowledge of God's forgiveness.

4 THE EVANGELICAL PRINCIPLE

60 *I think most Christians underestimate*: Glen Shellrude, in a personal email exchange.

65 *The purpose, center*: Christian Smith, *The Bible Made Impossible: Why Biblicism is Not a Truly Evangelical Reading of Scripture* (Grand Rapids: Brazos, 2011), 97.

67 *Faithful performances of Scripture*: Curtis W. Freeman, "Toward a *Sensus Fidelum* for an Evangelical Church: Postconervatives and Postliberals on Reading Scripture," in *The Nature of Confession: Evangelicals and Postliberals in Conversation*, ed. Timothy R. Phillip and Dennis L. Okholm (Downers Grove, IL: InterVarsity Press, 2007), 176.

5 THE SACRAMENTAL PRINCIPLE

84   *holiness and pentecostal traditions*: The anointing of the sick is also, of course, found within Anglican, Catholic, and other traditions.

On baptism: John Calvin, *Institutes of the Christian Religion, a New Translation by Henry Beveridge* (Edinburgh: Calvin Translation Society, 1845), 4.18.19.

Two sacraments: See Luther's *Babylonian Captivity of the Church* (published in 1520), *Works of Martin Luther*, vol. 2, translated by Albert T. W. Steinhaeuser (Philadelphia: A. J. Holman, 1915).

It belongs to the heart: Lesslie Newbigin, *The Household of God* (London: SCM Press, 1953), 77.

92   *The Spirit "overshadows" the bread and wine*: Rowan Williams, *Tokens of Trust: An Introduction to Christian Belief* (Louisville, KY: Westminster John Knox, 2007), 116-17.

We pray in the Holy Spirit: Ibid., 118.

The high moment in the celebration: Ibid., 117.

93   *Without active participation*: Simon Chan, "The Holy Spirit as the Fulfillment of the Liturgy," *Liturgy* 30.1 (2015): 33-41, 38.

6 THE PENTECOST PRINCIPLE

100   *Origen on participation in the life of God*: See especially *Spirit and Fire*. Origen and Hans Urs von Balthasar, *Origen, Spirit and Fire*, trans. Robert J. Daly S.J. (Washington, DC: Catholic University of America Press, 1984). All textual references that follow are to paragraph numbers in this edition.

Origen speaks of the "discernment of spirits": Ibid., paragraph 561.

His particular emphasis: Ibid., paragraph 566.

The resting place of the soul: Ibid., paragraphs 568-73.

101   *Peace not as a way of ease*: Ibid., paragraph 581.

An awareness of the love of God: Ibid., paragraph 584.

Feeling makes us wise: Bernard of Clairvaux, *Five Books on Consideration: Advice to a Pope*, trans. J. D. Anderson and E. T. Kennan (Kalamazoo,

MI: Cistercian Publications, 1976). See, for example, Sermons 23:14 and 16:1.

102 *Consolation and desolation*: See Louis J. Pohl, "Rules for Discernment," in *The Spiritual Exercises of St. Ignatius Loyola* (Allahabad: Saint Paul Society, 1975), 313-36.

106 *Feast of Pentecost in the early church*: Robert Louis Wilken, *The Spirit of Early Christian Thought: Seeking the Face of God* (New Haven, CT: Yale University Press, 2003), 103.

109 *Consolation without previous cause*: "The Second Rule," *Spiritual Exercises of St. Ignatius Loyola*, 313-36.

   The vital place of religious experience: Lesslie Newbigin, *The Household of God* (London: SCM Press, 1953), 91.

112 *John of the Cross could speak of the "dark night"*: The most important sources in this regard are the following: *The Ascent of Mount Carmel*; *The Dark Night* (which is essentially a continuation of the *Ascent*) and, *The Living Flame of Love*, all found in *The Collected Works of St. John of the Cross*, trans. by Kieran Kavanaugh and Otilio Rodriguez (Washington, DC: ICS Publications, 1979).

   The Christian a mystic: Karl Rahner, "Christian Living Formerly and Today," *Theological Investigations*, trans. David Bourke (New York: Herder and Herder, 1971), 7:15.

113 *Beginning with the work of the Spirit*: Elizabeth A. Johnson, *She Who Is: The Mystery of God in Feminist Theological Discourse* (New York: Crossroad, 1992).

118 *The Spirit can bypass the program*: Simon Chan, *Pentecostal Theology and the Christian Spiritual Tradition* (Sheffield: Sheffield Academic Press, 2000), see especially 38.

121 *Tension between institutional and charismatic church*: Karl Rahner, *The Dynamic Element in the Church* (Montreal: Palm Publishers, 1964), 48-51. Rahner's point is that the charismatic element in the church—the grace of the Holy Spirit—cannot be limited to the official, meaning for him sacramental, ministry of the church.

123 *Through our singing we enact the new community*: Steven R. Guthrie, *Creator Spirit: The Holy Spirit in the Art of Becoming Human* (Grand Rapids: Baker, 2011), 79-80.

GENERAL INDEX

anointing of the sick, 118
ascension, 5, 25, 26
Balthasar, Hans Urs von, 114
baptism, 17, 42, 66, 81, 85-86, 89, 90, 130
Bernard of Clairvaux, 101
Book of Common Prayer, 38
Calvin, John, 42, 44-46, 103
Chan, Simon, 117
chrismation, 124, 131
Christian initiation, 28
discernment, 29, 119-120
epiclēsis, 42, 92, 93
Eucharist. *See* Lord's Supper
Evangelical Theological Society, 52
Fee, Gordon, 121
filioque clause, 107-8
Guthrie, Steven R., 123
holy water, 95
Ignatius of Loyola, 99, 102, 103
incarnation, 79
Iona Community, 93
John of the Cross, 99, 102, 112
Johnson, Elizabeth A., 113
Jones, Scott, 48

Lord's Supper, 18, 33, 34, 38, 42, 86-88, 89, 90
Luther, Martin, 103
Manley Hopkins, Gerard, 114
Muntzer, Thomas, 103
Newbigin, Lesslie, 3, 109
Nicene Creed, 38, 107
Origen of Alexandria, 100
pilgrimage, 95
prayer for illumination, 69
Rahner, Karl, 112, 121
sign of the cross, 95
Smith, Christian, 65
Teresa of Avila, 99, 102
tongues-speaking, 122
union with Christ, 12
Welker, Michael, 4
Wesley, Charles, 99
Wesley, John, 42-50, 99
Wilken, Robert Thomas, 105
Williams, Rowan, 92
Wiman, Christopher, 39
Zwingli, Ulrich, 45

SCRIPTURE INDEX

ALSO AVAILABLE FROM
GORDON T. SMITH

Called to Be Saints

Courage & Calling

Consider Your Calling

Listening to God in Times of Choice

Spiritual Direction

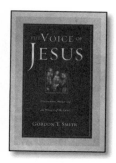

The Voice of Jesus

Finding the Textbook You Need

The IVP Academic Textbook Selector
is an online tool for instantly finding the IVP books
suitable for over 250 courses across 24 disciplines.

ivpacademic.com